The Man Who Is France

The Man
Who Is France

THE STORY OF GENERAL CHARLES DE GAULLE

By Stanley Clark

DODD, MEAD & COMPANY · NEW YORK · 1960

Preface

❧ I have found that most Frenchman are admirers of General Charles de Gaulle. There are perhaps millions who object to his policies—for he has no political label—and almost as many who find his austere outlook on life anathema. But almost every Frenchman admires and envies the single-mindedness of the President, and all, even the Communists, pay tribute to his honesty of purpose.

It was both easy and difficult to write this book. It was easy because there is so much color and incident in the life of de Gaulle, and difficult because it is not possible to pierce the barrier of anonymity which, despite the fact that he is so continually in the public eye, he has been able to erect round his life.

For the anecdotes in this book, as also for help in making its writing possible, I am indebted to a great many people. It would be impossible to mention every one by name, but among those to whom I must express gratitude are M. Jacques Soustelle, Minister Delegate attached to the (French) Prime Minister's Office; Baron Olivier Guichard, the *Directeur Adjoint* of the Cabinet; M. Claude Bouchinet-Serreulles; M. Georges Boris; M. Rémy Roure, the distinguished writer; and M. Charles Ronsac, editor of *Opera Mundi*.

S. C.

Contents

Contents

The Man Who Is France

1

Return to Power

❖ General de Gaulle drove out of the closely guarded gates of the Hôtel Matignon, the vast mansion in the rue de Varennes, where Talleyrand, the famous eighteenth-century diplomat, once lived, and where now the Presidents of the Council of France have their official residence and offices. The bereted Frenchman beside me said sideways from the corner of his mouth, "If only de Gaulle had some little human weaknesses the world would consider him greater even than Churchill."

It was September 1958. For four months General Charles de Gaulle had been at the Matignon, directing the destiny of France. Swept back to power on June 1 by an incredible bloodless revolution, he had taken up the direction of the country as if from the point where he had left off when he resigned in January 1946. He had come back as if hesitantly, though he had long planned just such a dramatic return to the seat of power; he had shown France that he was still capable of standing aloof if the conditions under which he would hold power were not to his liking; he had demonstrated that power for power's sake had no appeal for him. He had revealed to his fellow-countrymen once more the almost unbelievable singlemindedness of his life and his aspirations. He had imposed his will upon France by insisting that France must call for him before he would move from retirement.

1

Though he had apparently not sought power, here he was in the leadership of France again. After little more than a fortnight of tension and excitement in May he had turned a hostile National Assembly into one which asked for his return; a country which was not completely convinced that he was not at heart a Fascist into one which gave him an overwhelming vote of confidence at a free and unequivocal referendum.

As he drove out through the gates on that sunny September day, and the chains which bar the passage of all cars into the great courtyard of the Hôtel Matignon were pulled up behind him, there was nothing in his cold, impassive face to reveal the extraordinary power of this man. The small crowd which watched in silence seemed to search for an act, a mannerism, which would tell them that he was human after all. Charles de Gaulle would be colorless if he were not France itself. For that is how he thinks of himself and how the people now increasingly think of him.

How much was he behind the events of the fateful afternoon of May 13, 1958, when an excited crowd besieged the offices of the Minister for Algeria in Algiers and proclaimed the formation of a Committee of Public Safety? De Gaulle was behind the entire movement, yet in fact he had no part in it. Though he did not know that a *coup d'état* was to take place that afternoon, he was fully aware that his close followers and the millions who supported him in France and in the French Union overseas were demanding action and determined to take power into their own hands if it became evident that only in that way could France be saved.

The famous commander of the parachutists, General Massu, who seized power in Algiers on May 13, was a

Gaullist supporter. He had been in constant touch with de Gaulle in the years when the latter had appeared to be in retirement, as had other famous French soldiers—Juin, Koenig, Salan. Massu had been in command of French paratroops in the abortive operations against Egypt in 1956. When ordered to retire he had declared, "This is the last time I shall obey an order like that."

In Algiers, Massu and all who helped him were carrying out the de Gaulle plan just as surely as if the General had been directing operations in person. The plan for Algeria which was adopted immediately de Gaulle returned to power was not new: the General's supporters had revealed almost every detail of it in the two years previously. And de Gaulle had never divorced himself for one moment from the very friends who called for his return. Yet he held himself aloof from every one so far as action was concerned.

De Gaulle had always made it plain that he would not take power save by the obvious and overwhelming desire of the French people. Though he despised the French Constitution because he believed it was ruining France, he would do nothing that would destroy it illegally. Not for one instant did he depart from his stated position: "I will return to power only if called back by France."

When Massu, immediately on his formation of the Committee of Public Safety in Algiers, addressed a call to the President of France, René Coty, to invite de Gaulle to take up office as President of the Council, de Gaulle made no move. He was well aware that everything was moving his way, and that he could afford to wait. The people at home had grown tired of the constant succession of Governments—twenty-five Cabinets since the war and seventeen Presidents of the Council—none of which had done any-

thing to restore the position of France as a World Power
or to improve the economic position of the country. French
men and women had grown cynical at the political de-
cadence at home: their jokes at the cost of their high living
standards had more than a little despair in them. "One
child means nothing," they would say. "Two children
mean a vacuum-cleaner, three a refrigerator. When you
have four you can run a small car, and with five, so long
as you sell the small car, you can run a Rolls-Royce."

In Algeria the colonists, as well as a majority of the
Muslim population, had grown weary of the long years of
war, and the Army too, with four years of constant ambush
in Algeria following eight years of death, disease, and
despair in Indo-China, was ripe for change. All sections of
the people felt that France was about to give way once
more to the pressure of her Allies—America and Britain—
to sacrifice herself and her possessions on the altar of Arab
appeasement.

De Gaulle had never really retired from politics when he
gave up power on January 20, 1946, and went to live, first
in the State-owned lodge at Marly-le-Roi, thirty miles outside Paris, and later at his own home at Colombey-les-
Deux-Eglises. With consummate skill he, and his associates, gave the impression that he had done so—even
helped to enlarge the myth of the hermit of Colombey—
while in fact he and they were working, planning, and preparing, releasing carefully thought-out statements and
comments from time to time and making sure that in the
minds of all people the inevitability of de Gaulle's return
was firmly implanted. But there were times when even the
patient General began to feel that too long had elapsed
since he retired from politics for there to be any hope of a
recall. "I am afraid it is too late," he told a friend in Janu-

ary 1958. "Even if the people have not forgotten me they have lost the need for me."

It was in February of that year that political observers in France noticed a sudden and big increase in the number of visitors—politicians, trade-union leaders, and high-ranking army officers. Gaston Palewski, General Koenig, Mendès-France, Soustelle, Delbecque, Juin—these were only a few who then saw the General at Colombey, at his Paris hotel (La Pérouse, in the rue La Pérouse, close to the Etoile, which he always visited once a week), or at his offices (never closed throughout the years of apparent inaction) in the rue de Solférino. Yet these discussions never gave rise to any undue suspicion that a come-back was planned. Throughout France, however, a whispering campaign was started up, and *"de Gaulle au pouvoir!"* was heard with greater and greater frequency.

Jacques Soustelle, always the mouthpiece for Gaullist theories in the French Parliament, overthrew, or was chiefly responsible for the overthrow of, the Government of Félix Gaillard on April 16, after a decision to put the de Gaulle plan into operation had been arrived at. Soustelle immediately called for an invitation to de Gaulle to return to power. This was no spur-of-the-moment thought, and it achieved its objective, for throughout France and outside its borders people began to discuss the possibility of such a happening, though few of those best in the know gave him much chance of success. De Gaulle himself made no comment of any kind. He paid even closer attention to the situation reports which now came each day to his desk, and issued the necessary directions to deal with every changed circumstance.

Two days after Soustelle's call for de Gaulle the Association of Free Frenchmen openly demanded his return, and

on April 28 a gathering of Breton fishermen sent a petition
to President Coty asking him to invite de Gaulle to form
a Government. But these, though they might be straws in
the wind, still seemed to observers to be more like chaff.

What would have been a more active pointer to the
imminence of action would have been the revelation of
the number of Gaullist supporters who were making the
trip to Algeria to observe conditions there and to discuss
the remedies with supporters. There were many such
visits, but no observer was sufficiently watchful either to
take notice of them or to comment on them, and for once
the highly efficient publicity machine of de Gaulle, oper-
ated by Soustelle, was still and silent.

One of the principal figures in the Algerian scene was
Alain de Sérigny, editor of the important daily newspaper
L'Echo d'Alger. He was a militant campaigner for action
against the terrorists, and for decisive efforts to ensure that
Algeria should remain French. Sérigny came to Paris, unnoticed by members of the press, on May 8, and spent the
entire time there with Soustelle and Léon Delbecque, a
famous member of the wartime Resistance in France and
a Member of the National Assembly. Delbecque had
served in Algeria, and knew the problems that France
faced there. He was also a Gaullist.

At this meeting the final plans for action in Algeria
which would result in the recall of de Gaulle were discussed. But there was still no question of a *coup d'état*.
The conspirators agreed that Sérigny and Delbecque
should travel to Algeria and there attempt to persuade
Robert Lacoste, the Governor-General, to agree to ask
President Coty to invite de Gaulle to return to office. They
were disturbed that Pierre Pflimlin was in Paris attempting
to form a Ministry, and feared that if he succeeded he

might weld the great parties in Parliament into a sufficiently unanimous whole to remain in power for weeks, if not months, and thus make it impossible for any open call to go out for de Gaulle until it was too late for him to do anything to save the situation for France. They were certain that matters were as serious as that, and that only the immediate return of the General could save the country from disaster.

But Lacoste would not listen to the arguments of the two envoys. In typical conspiratorial fashion, Soustelle, Sérigny, and Delbecque had arranged a series of code messages which would convey the position to one another without giving rise to suspicion in Paris or Algiers. When the French Ministry in Algiers agreed to support de Gaulle, Sérigny would send, "My Editor-in-Chief likes your article and will publish it to-day." But though that message was never sent, a new and powerful ally came into the picture. General Salan, Commander-in-Chief of all French forces in Algeria, who was in complete agreement with Sérigny, sent a message to President Coty in which he warned of the disquieting attitude of his men, who were demanding that something positive be done in Algeria and that a Government resolved to carry out a strong policy which would keep France in Algeria should be formed in Paris. Salan appealed to the President to take action on his message, pointing out that it was not like the army to take matters into its own hands in this way, which revealed the seriousness of the situation.

This was the chance that Sérigny and Delbecque had waited for: it was as strong a card as an appeal by Lacoste, perhaps stronger. They hurried back to Paris, and immediately went into conference with Soustelle. They were sure that the Army in Algeria could be relied upon *en masse* to support de Gaulle. Officers and men alike had had too many experiences of terrorists, who attacked always with stealth and treachery, to have second thoughts in this direction. So many of them had lost relatives in the fighting and were boiling for revenge and for victory, which would be as sweet as revenge. As for the colonists, there could be no doubt on whose side they would be, despite the fact that Sérigny, their leading spokesman, had not always been a Gaullist. He had, in fact, taunted de Gaulle in 1945 with having been the man who introduced the first Communist, Maurice Thorez, into the Government of France, and pointed out that it had taken a Socialist, Paul Ramadier, to remove him from it again. But now Sérigny was firmly behind the one man whom he knew could carry the day.

De Gaulle still refused to alter the stand he had taken from the start. He would consent to take power only if he knew that all France wanted him back.

The efforts of Sérigny and Delbecque became known to the Government in Paris, and orders were given that the former should be arrested. But on May 12 he managed to board a plane, which carried him back to Algiers safely, ready for—indeed, determined on—the course to be adopted on the following day. Delbecque, after some thought, followed him, and they were both on hand when the Committee of Public Safety was set up. Soustelle decided that he could best serve the situation by remaining in Paris, where he could play his part in the National Assembly when the crucial vote was taken on Pflimlin's administration. The announcement of the formation of the Committee of Public Safety took matters out of his hands, however, for Pflimlin easily obtained his vote from an Assembly which was by then really frightened for the fate of the Fourth Republic.

There were stories that the Army in Algeria was ready to march on France itself, and that parachutists were about to float down on Paris to take over all the key points. The Government acted swiftly in ensuring that the police and the security police were ready. General Paul Ely, French Chief of the General Staff, resigned, and there were immediately rumors that many high-ranking officers had been arrested—all untrue, but they added to the atmosphere of uncertainty and confusion. The Army in Metropolitan France was confined to barracks. Yet life in city and countryside went on calmly and apparently normally.

Soustelle was placed under nominal house arrest. The strong guard of metropolitan police and the Compagnies Républicaines de Sécurité placed around his Paris house may certainly have been there only to guard him against action by Algerian terrorists, but it also effectively prevented him from moving out to further his plans and those of his chief.

Here was a situation made for the wartime chief of the Free French Intelligence Service. In the evening of May 14 Geoffroy de la Tour du Pin, a staunch Gaullist, drove up to the Soustelle home in the Avenue Henri-Martin. The police admitted him, and the visitor drove his car into the courtyard, stopped it in front of the door, and switched off his lights. In a few moments he was admitted to the house, and the yard lights were switched off. Almost at once, under cover of the darkness, Soustelle slipped out of the house and climbed into the trunk of the car, letting the cover down after him. La Tour du Pin came out of the house soon after and got behind the wheel of his car. At the gate the police examined the interior of the car, saw that it contained only the driver, and allowed it to pass.

La Tour du Pin drove out of Paris. At a suburban airfield Soustelle got out from the trunk and boarded a light aircraft, which had been hired from a Swiss company by a friend, General Pierre de Benonville, editor of a Paris periodical. When the plane took off for Algeria, Benonville travelled with Soustelle.

In Algiers, Soustelle, as former Resident Minister, was given a welcome bordering on the delirious. Almost a third of the population of the city, Muslim as well as European, turned out to greet him, and the cries of "Soustelle, Soustelle!" were mingled with those of "De Gaulle!"

The confusion that reigned in Paris, while on the surface confined to political circles, was as great as could be. De Gaulle had arrived in the capital and installed himself at the Hôtel La Pérouse on May 14, and on the following day he issued a brief statement to the Press:

> The degradation of the State inevitably brings with it the estrangement of the associated peoples, trouble in the Army in the field, national dislocation, the loss of independence. For the past twelve years France, at grips with problems too great for the party regime, has been engaged in this disastrous process. In the past the country, in its depths, placed its confidence in me to lead it wholly to its salvation.
>
> To-day, in the face of the new difficulties which are mounting towards it, let the country know that I hold myself ready to assume the powers of the Republic.

This was the real de Gaulle—confident to the point of egotism. His remarks brought an outburst of anger from the Left and calls for national strikes. There were jubilant demands for his return from his own supporters.

The Government retaliated by declaring a State of Emergency on May 16, which gave the Minister of the Interior powers to forbid the movement of people and vehicles; establish security zones in which people's residence could be regulated; order people who tried to hamper the action of the public authorities to leave any place; order house searches at any time; institute censorship of press, radio, cinema, and theater; ban gatherings and order bars and places of entertainment to be closed; order a curfew and set up banned areas.

Now listeners to French and Algerian radio stations (and that meant every one in both France and Algeria) began to notice the strangest interruptions to their programs. In the middle of one program a voice declared, "The Palm is in the Oasis." It was admitted that the message had been sent at the order of the French Ministry of Information: it told the Committee of Public Safety in Algiers that de Gaulle had come to Paris to consult the Government. Soon Algiers Radio was answering, "The Chapel will be lit up to-night," signifying that the Committee would wait to hear the results of the discussions.

It now seemed certain in the minds of most people that the Army in Algeria was becoming impatient, and there were more stories of an imminent parachute attack on the capital. De Gaulle saw in this threat a certainty of civil war and a possible postponement, if not cancellation, of all his plans. Civil war must be averted at all costs, for that would indeed bring France to her knees. He called a press conference, and on May 19, in the Hôtel Palais d'Orsay, which was heavily guarded by many squads of riot police, he made a considered statement.

The General said that the assumption of the powers of the Republic (to which he had previously referred) could be made in those exceptional moments and for an exceptional task only through an exceptional procedure for investiture by the National Assembly. "In the circumstances such an investiture could not take place according to the usual rites and procedures which everybody is sick of," he said.

"The population of Algeria has despaired of obtaining

a solution of its problems from what I call 'The System' in Paris, and I ask you, 'How could people not revolt in these circumstances?'

"The population of Algeria does not want to be separated from France. You do not cry 'Long live de Gaulle!' if you are not on the side of France.

"There has been talk of seditious generals, but no sanctions are taken against them by the public powers. I am not the public powers. Why should I say they are seditious? I am a man who belongs to no one and to every one," he said.

When asked what he meant by "assuming the powers of the Republic," the General replied, "The powers of the Republic can only be those which the Republic delegates.

"The danger is that solutions will finally be forced upon France, and they will be, without doubt, the worst possible.

"There was a time when the Republic was rejected.

"I have restored her arms and her name and led her to victory with all those who willingly wanted to join me."

When he had finished his speech de Gaulle said simply, "I shall now go back to my village and there hold myself at the disposal of the country."

As he walked back through the crowd to his car, which drove him to his offices in the rue de Solférino, there could be no doubt that he was winning his battle. The streets were crowded with people, and the cries of "De Gaulle!" were almost unanimous.

De Gaulle had spoken to Algeria and stilled the fears of the Committee of Public Safety. He had spoken to France and partially stilled the fears of those who felt he was about to seize power. His calming words averted a real threat of civil war.

Four days later Antoine Pinay, the leader of the Independents, drove from Paris to Colombey to see the General. Pierre Pflimlin, the President of the Council, stressed that this visit was unofficial and entirely Pinay's idea, but few people really believed this, especially when Pinay saw Pflimlin immediately on his return to Paris. But before anything concrete could come out of the meeting the Committee of Public Safety struck again, this time in Ajaccio, Corsica, where parachutists took over power. The Marines were ordered to dislodge them and take control of the island, but they refused, and they were also joined by the police.

In Paris the attempts to mobilize the workers failed signally. In the great Renault works, where it was thought the Communists might have tremendous support, the response was almost nonexistent. And though there were some stoppages of work, in the main life flowed without pause, and certainly with little out-of-the-ordinary incident. Paris was calm.

The Government realized that the end was in sight for them, if not for the Fourth Republic itself. There were many hurried meetings between the leading politicians. Guy Mollet, Robert Schuman, Pinay—all saw de Gaulle's aides and discussed the next moves. On May 26 a packed National Assembly heard that the General was conferring with President Coty and Pflimlin in the Château de Champs, part of the Prime Minister's office and lying east of the city. The following midday de Gaulle issued a statement that he was "engaged on the regular procedure necessary to the establishment of a Republican Government." Not even Frenchmen understood what he meant.

What was not apparent was that de Gaulle had once more had his hand forced by threats of strikes at home and action by the paratroops in Algeria, who threatened to drop on Paris that same evening unless he was called back. Supporters in Paris were ready to join with them with small arms and grenades, and civil war was again very near that day.

Once more the General's statement calmed both sides, or at least gave them pause.

Leading Frenchmen of all political views except the extreme Left now began to call for the General's return. Vincent Auriol, a well-loved ex-President of France, was not least in appealing to President Coty. And, finally, Pinay persuaded the President that no other course remained.

The President's appeal to the National Assembly to vote de Gaulle into power succeeded on June 1, and France breathed again.

For General Charles de Gaulle it was the culmination of one of the longest and most difficult and complicated strategical and tactical exercises he had ever conducted. He had planned for his return with the care and the ice-cold reasoning he always gave to his military exercises and real-life campaigns, and against opponents who could do no more than improvise from day to day he had a decided advantage. But he had also shown a deep insight into the character of his countrymen, and a patience that surprised even those who had known the de Gaulle patience of old. He had shown his own people, too, a little more clearly that in himself de Gaulle sees all France.

On June 1, 1958, the greatest phase of de Gaulle's life began.

2

De Gaulle in the Story of France

❦ A Frenchman who is also a fervent admirer of de Gaulle has summed up his character in these words: "When General de Gaulle wants to consult a map of France he looks in his mirror." That description is apt. For all his life de Gaulle has identified himself—and only partly because of his name—with everything that is France.

He was born at Lille in the home of his grandfather, Jules Maillot-Delannoy, at 9 rue Princesse, on November 22, 1890, but he grew up in Paris, where his father, Henri de Gaulle, after first-class service in the French Army, became, in 1901, Professor of Philosophy, Mathematics, and Literature in the Jesuit College in the rue de Vaugirard. Henri de Gaulle was a staunch Catholic, and it was the law depriving the religious orders of the right to teach in schools which persuaded him to throw up a career in the army, although he had set his heart on it, to offer his services to the Jesuit Fathers. It was his method of protesting against a law which he always argued fiercely was both unjust and damaging to France. But it was a sad decision to make, and he never ceased to be drawn towards all matters military.

Henri de Gaulle fought with some distinction in the Franco-Prussian War of 1870-71; he was in the Mobiles de la Seine, and was wounded at the battle at Le Bourget

15

during the siege of Paris, where the war had finally come
to an end. He was later promoted to the rank of colonel,
and it then seemed that his army career was established.
Luckily, when he came to his great decision in regard to
the Jesuit College, he could also claim to be a graduate
of the Ecole Polytechnique in Paris, and that made his
transfer easier.

Charles de Gaulle grew up in an atmosphere that was
as much religious as it was military. His mother, Jeanne
Maillot, came of a military and literary family which had
first been linked with the de Gaulles early in the nine-
teenth century. Young Charles received from his earliest
years an intensive religious education, which was inter-
spersed frequently with weighty discussions on military
affairs and discourses on the honor of France, which, in
most families outside France, might have been considered
out of place in the upbringing of one so young. But the de
Gaulles have been prominently identified with the story
of France for many centuries: they were among the leading families of Normandy in the Middle Ages, and Jean de
Gaulle was one of the French noblemen at the battle of
Agincourt. It is said that at that time he attempted to warn
the Constable d'Albret, who commanded the French
Army, that the heavy ground placed the French at a dis-
advantage compared to the mobile English archers, but
his advice was disregarded. If true, the story was to be
repeated by Charles de Gaulle five hundred years later.
Seigneur de Gaulle, head of the family, was one of the
lieutenants of Charles VI of France, and he was given the
honor of defending the Porte Saint-Denis against the attacking forces of Burgundy in 1414. After the victory of
Henry V in Normandy, Jean de Gaulle refused to take the
oath of allegiance to the English king, and his goods and

lands were confiscated. He was rewarded by the King of France with a fief of land in Cuisery, in Burgundy, in recompense for his military service. Later the family transferred to Dijon, where they entered the Parliament of Burgundy. They moved finally to Paris in the eighteenth century, where they entered the law.

Henri de Gaulle often talked of the eagerness with which his son Charles learned these stories from the past. "He was a child wise beyond his years," he said. "Almost involuntarily one found oneself discussing with him events and subjects that one would have imagined were beyond his comprehension."

Charles de Gaulle was reading the history of France before he was five years old. Soon the *Chronicles* of Froissart, the medieval historian, were his favorite reading, and from them, and the gradual understanding of the significance of his name, there developed a devouring interest in and attachment for France herself. He showed an instinctive desire to understand the past of France and to recreate her glories in his own time.

It was with a breathless interest in the excitement of battle that he first read history. It was the battles that France had fought that first gripped his attention. Very soon he was astonishing his elders by his analyses of battle strategy. His father has said of him that he could formulate an appreciation of a military campaign before he seriously commenced his schooling.

Yet at first he had wanted to be a missionary in one of France's underdeveloped overseas territories, and when, as a child, he was taken by his parents to Mass in Notre-Dame the beauty of the great cathedral impressed him more than anything he had seen. It became one of his favorite excursions: the view from the top of the towers

never ceased to thrill him, and other favorites were the
thirteenth-century frescoes behind the choir, which were
restored by a namesake of his mother. But his nearest
church when he was in Paris was Saint-Sulpice, where he
used to be taken to listen to the wonderful organ music.
And from there he was able to visit the Palais de Luxembourg, where his great-great-grandfather, Jean-Baptiste,
worked with Louis XVI at the time of the French Revolution, and was imprisoned there for his loyalty. But often
in his childhood he lived in Lille, and there the famous
cathedral drew him just as strongly as Notre-Dame.

Charles discovered one day his great-grandfather's *Nou-
velle histoire de Paris,* and this fired him afresh with a
desire to know the city and its environs. Gradually the
familiar landmarks became for him the background to his
dreams—the Cathedral of Notre-Dame, Les Invalides, Ver-
sailles, the Luxembourg, the Arc de Triomphe, the Abby of
Saint-Denis, of which he had read in the *Vie de St. Louis,*
also written by his great-grandfather. He has many times
admitted that nothing in his childhood made a greater
and more lasting impression on him than these symbols of
the past glories of France. But in them also he was seeing a
vivid patchwork of the errors and failings of his country, at
first unrealized in the child mind, but developing none the
less.

His mother led him gradually to a facility in writing
through the example of his ancestors—Julien-Philippe de
Gaulle, who had married her own grandmother Maillot,
and Mme. Julien-Philippe, who wrote a life of Daniel
O'Connell, liberator of Ireland, and a life of Chateaubriand. These two books impressed Charles very much.
O'Connell's character fascinated him, and the Irishman's
lifelong fight for the rights of the Catholic religion and for

the freedom of his native land stirred him to admiration. As a boy he would often cite the example of O'Connell when he wished to make a point of resistance to some injustice. And in Chateaubriand he found a man whose life was to provide an extraordinarily close model for his own. He did not admire Chateaubriand's lukewarm adherence to his religion, but the famous man's *Le Génie du christianisme* had a profound effect on his own literary style.

It was from the Maillot side of the family that Charles inherited the height which was later to earn him the nickname of "La Grande Asperge." The Maillots also gave him an exceptional self-control and his wonderful powers of endurance, owing, it is said, with graceful tribute to the Irish and Scots, to the marriage of his mother's grandfather with Julia Delannoy, a woman of mixed Irish-Scots ancestry. De Gaulle's mother was fond of telling her son of the Celtic origin of the de Gaulles, and introduced him at an early age to the book written by his uncle, the first Charles de Gaulle, entitled, *Les Celtes au XIXe siècle,* which advocated a union of the Breton, Scots, Irish, and Welsh.

Among the works of his uncle there is found a passage which the younger man had always carried with him as encouragement: "When an army is overrun by a surprise attack no one questions the rank or the right of the man who raises the flag again and utters the first call to resistance." That message Charles de Gaulle II had on his desk at school. Nothing could have been more prophetic.

As soon as he was able to understand, young Charles de Gaulle began to worry over the reverses of France in the war of 1870 with Germany. He began to question his father on the events of the war—the bad handling by

Marshal Bazaine of his army at Vionville, Mars-la-Tour, and Gravelotte, and the failure of Marshal MacMahon to take advantage of his superiority over the Crown Prince of Prussia, and thus to relieve Bazaine, by then beleaguered at Metz. Charles de Gaulle knew all the details of the capitulation at Sedan and at Metz, and finally of the surrender of Paris. His own father had been wounded in that last great siege, and could provide a graphic description of conditions in the city at that time. The boy read in detail of the engagements which had preceded the fall of Sedan— of the fierce battle between the Uhlans of the Army of the Meuse and of the French Chasseurs Alpins which had finally let the German Army through to overrun Mac-Mahon, and so led to the fall of Sedan, the traditional gateway to France from the east.

It was now that the boy began to reveal his intense interest in military matters. He played soldiers as readily as other boys did, but he played them not as a rough-and-ready game, but as a serious essay in military science. Before he was ten he was organizing the youth of the neighborhood, including his elder brother, Xavier, and his younger brothers, Jacques and Pierre, in fierce battles against the enemy, and he showed a catholic taste in enemies. Thus the result of Agincourt was reversed because Charles de Gaulle had recognized the faults of French tactics and had deployed his superior forces more thinly than had the Constable d'Albret, thus preventing the easy triumph of the English archers. He was then the embodiment of Jean de Gaulle. Another time he defended again the Porte Saint-Denis against the Duke of Burgundy, and he was Joan of Arc through all her campaigns. He was the great sailor Jean Bart, and sailed to adventure in the same way as that famous admiral of Louis XIV; he was the Jean-Baptiste de Gaulle, not the King's advocate, but the eighteenth-century engineer who built the wharves and lighthouses of Le Havre and turned it into France's greatest northern port. And sometimes he was Charles Maillot, the artilleryman of the Franco-Prussian War, or Jean Maillot, the man who had built the fortifications of Lille for Seigneur de Vauban, the seventeenth-century military engineer who gave the world a new conception of the art of fortification. The work of Vauban was something for young Charles de Gaulle to study, and to analyze. He stored away his memories and his conclusions for more than a quarter of a century, and then used them to demonstrate the futility of France's relying almost entirely on the Maginot Line for her defense against aggression from the east.

His father and mother, though they often expressed astonishment at his earnestness, yet found no signs of precocity in him. That is also the opinion of his contemporaries. He was by nature reserved, almost shy. Yet at ten years of age he was taking command, real command, of boys four and five years his senior, and they were obeying his orders without question. It was not only that he was so tall, that he looked older than they, nor that his knowledge of all the games they played lifted him out of their class. He had an instinctive and powerful gift of leadership.

Henri de Gaulle was himself a man of great character. In addition to teaching in the Jesuit College, he taught in a school in the rue des Postes, where boys were sent who later were destined for the Ecole Polytechnique or Saint-Cyr. Here he had among his scholars not only his son, Charles, but others who were to become famous in French military history, Guynemer, the airman, and de Lattre de Tassigny, who found fame in Indo-China, being among them.

The de Gaulle household was always unpretentious, per-

haps even a little austere. Charles grew up in an atmosphere of planned frugality, and the habits he acquired
then have never left him. Henri de Gaulle did not believe
in luxuries. Occasionally he would take his family to a
theater to see some classic play—*Le Bourgeois gentil-
homme* was one of Charles's favorites—but otherwise their
recreation was found in the home in good books and
sparkling conversation. Henri had a wide circle of friends,
and many were important figures in French public life.
Charles met and talked with them all.

From their earliest days Henri had made it a habit to
talk to his children in as adult a way as they could comprehend. He was firm with them but affectionate to a degree,
and he was immensely popular with them all. Yet as the
years passed he found himself drawn closer and closer to
Charles, in whom both he and his wife saw one who could
translate all their dreams for France into reality. Henri
and Jeanne de Gaulle were incurable romantics.

Charles de Gaulle was set on his course from the age
when he first could walk. Impressed immediately with
the significance of his name, he was next tutored in the
service his family had given to France down the centuries,
and then in the lives of the great men who had gone before
and left their mark on the nation's life. Thus when the
dreamer Charles played at being Richelieu, Louis XIV,
Joan of Arc, Chateaubriand, Napoleon Bonaparte—particularly Napoleon—his mother and father made no demur.
They seemed to know that in him was developing the Man
of France. "From such a child as he we expect much," his
father said when the boy was no more than eight years old.

3

No Stripes for Private de Gaulle

❧ Charles de Gaulle was thirteen years of age when one day in late spring he asked his father if he would allow him to organize a boy's camp in the Dordogne, where the family planned to spend their summer holidays. His father hesitated no more than momentarily though he had planned a very different vacation. And for the next few weeks he looked on with quiet amusement, soon mixed with proud admiration, at the way in which his son was preparing the campaign.

When, finally, the family set out for Ligerie, in the Dordogne, which was to be their headquarters, everything was arranged with the meticulous care of a military exercise. Charles carried with him his favorite *History of France,* from which he planned to extract many of the games he was preparing for the young campers. Theirs was a movable camp, marching from village to village like an army on the move, and only the onset of the wheat and wine harvests, which made it necessary for the local farmers to call on all their young helpers, broke it up.

Charles was disappointed at such an early end to his camp, but he proceeded to organize his own holiday. And his young campers had by then fought again half a score of the famous battles of France—and all to the de Gaulle plan.

Charles had always had an interest in the French Gen-

eral Louis Faidherbe, whose birthplace was only a stone's
throw from where Charles had been born in Lille. He made
a detailed study of the bloody but indecisive battles of
the 1870 campaign in Northern France, when Faidherbe
tried desperately to halt the advancing troops of Man-
teuffel and Goeben. He analyzed the reasons for Faidherbe's lack of success, and replanned the battles so
carefully that his plans were models of their kind. "Charles
was not satisfied merely to play soldiers," said one of his
childhood friends. "His battles had to be the real thing,
with properly drawn-up plans, and strategy and tactics
playing their part."

But by now Charles was developing as a scholar. His inherited skill as a writer was not so apparent at first, for he
contributed to literary reviews under pseudonyms. As he
got into his teens he began to take a great interest in
the writing of Shakespeare and Goethe, as well as of
French writers, including Montaigne (the *Essays* were
among his favorite reading), Sébastien-Roch Chamfort
("Chamfortiana"), Blaise Pascal (*Pensées sur la religion et
sur quelques autres sujets* and *Apologie de la religion
chrétienne*), and, again, Chateaubriand. Charles studied
astronomy until he could pick out most of the important
stars of the night sky in any month. And he still continued
to read every history of France, or any that had a close
connection with France, that he came upon.

His father's interest in philosophy was very early transmitted to the boy. Charles read Socrates and Plato, and
studied Kant's *Critique of Pure Reason* as much to obtain a
critical survey of himself as for any real love for the
work. He was drawn to the German philosopher's theory
that the three original faculties which enable man to
acquire knowledge are sense, understanding, and reason.

In his father's extensive library he found the works of Friedrich Nietzsche, and he was reading them at an age when most boys would have found them far beyond their comprehension. He was intrigued by Nietzsche's theories—the desire of man to obtain power and to dominate all obstacles. Nietzsche's developing theory of the Master Race, which would provide the aristocracy of the future, was not lost on the boy. "Is this the reason why Germany aimed to spread out to the west and came into conflict with France?" he asked his father. Charles was to remember all that he had read of Nietzsche many times during the next half-century of his life.

But it was the French philosophers—Descartes and Bergson, the latter an older contemporary of his—who exercised the greatest influence on the boy. Bergson's theory of duration and movement attracted Charles, and "I am a being which endures" was a belief after his own heart. Bergson was indeed friendly towards Charles, and many times talked to him during his visits to the de Gaulle home.

How far he was influenced by Bergson's theory that philosophy, like science, can progress only by devoting itself to individual problems, instead of advancing general theories and universal systems, it is difficult to say. But certainly de Gaulle has always approached every problem of his life as a separate and possibly unique situation demanding a plan and an attack of its own. Bergson's admonition that man should strive after a precise adaptation to reality also appealed to young de Gaulle, and the philosopher's belief that the true nature of things can be understood best by intuition made absolute sense to him.

These principles have colored and affected his life to a remarkable degree. It was perhaps to his father and to Henri Bergson that Charles de Gaulle owed most in the molding of his character. And Bergson, who died in 1941 at more than eighty years of age, must have felt that he had molded well, for he declared for de Gaulle in 1940. Yet, despite the almost frightening erudition of the young Charles, all who knew him in those days tell of the love he had for practical jokes: "fiendishly ingenious" is how they have been described. No one was safe, not even his father and mother, but they paid tribute to the fact that, disconcerting as they sometimes were, his jokes were never cruel and rarely embarrassing. His booby traps, which he delighted in placing all over the house, were ingenious and usually startling rather than damaging.

On one occasion the household in Paris was put into a high state of excitement over the supposed arrival of "General Faidherbe." The servants set about their preparations in a fever of anxiety, made all the more intense by the belief that it was a visit which had to be kept secret from Henri de Gaulle and his wife. Young Charles cleverly kept the secret even when his father and mother sensed there was something afoot by binding each to secrecy with the assurance that it was to be a surprise for the other. When at last the moment for the visit arrived, and every one, including the mystified Henri and Jeanne de Gaulle, was waiting for the visitor to put in an appearance, "General Faidherbe," in the person of Charles de Gaulle, came on the scene, a broad smile of triumphant delight on his face.

Henri de Gaulle spent as much time as he could in guiding and developing the education of his second son, whose tastes were so close to his own. And when, in the early years of the new century, Franco-German relations again became strained father and son came even closer together in their anxiety for the future. Henri did not see anything strange in discussing with his young son the involved process of the Dreyfus case, and whether Captain Dreyfus in fact had been guilty of espionage on behalf of Germany. Charles was fifteen when the case was reopened and Dreyfus had his sentence annulled. The repercussions of this case and the closeness that France had come to revolution over its scandals created an impression on young de Gaulle. And the fact that anyone could be sentenced on false evidence horrified him. He had always had a strong love of freedom and justice, and this no doubt came from his father's own experiences.

By now Charles had firmly decided that he would be a soldier. The influence of Faidherbe, who, despite his lack of positive success against the Germans, had given France a vast new colonial empire, was possibly decisive at that time, but another factor was the dangers threatening his country from without and within. He felt, and he never altered his opinion, that France must always be strong if she is to live.

It was in August 1909 that Charles de Gaulle left the school in the rue des Postes and entered the military college of Saint-Cyr. The rule had just been made that every cadet officer for Saint-Cyr must first undergo a year of military service as a soldier in the ranks.

Charles de Gaulle chose the 33rd Regiment of Infantry, and in due course arrived at Arras and reported to the barracks there. He was allotted to the company of Captain F. de Tugny. There was to follow a year which neither Tugny nor de Gaulle ever forgot. It led to a slightly bewildered de Tugny declaring, when asked why he had never recommended Private de Gaulle for a stripe, "What use to make that young man a sergeant when the only military title that would interest him would be High

Constable [the highest rank in the France of olden times]?"

De Gaulle did not at first give any indication that he would become even a good soldier, let alone a great one. His sergeant described him as being untidy, and hardly a day passed without the young man's being pulled up for some error of dress or deportment. His pack was rarely made up to the satisfaction of the meticulous sergeant, and that fellow delighted in pulling it roughly apart and telling de Gaulle to remake it before inspection. At other times it was some fault in the uniform or in the hair or in the method of standing on parade. "Le Grand Charles" was certainly a safety valve for the rest of his comrades.

De Gaulle was already rebelling against what he considered to be the nonessentials of Army life. It was not that he was against smartness or discipline; only that he felt that much of what the Army regarded as smartness and discipline was merely time-wasting, irritating, and therefore destructive of the best material in the Army. De Gaulle believed in the idea that a soldier should be highly trained in the art of war; he believed that the art of war was continually changing, and that Army drill and training must change at the same pace. The drill of 1870 and the same barracks discipline could never suit the modern Army, he argued.

At Arras he was known as a lonely, unsociable soldier, one who rarely mixed with his comrades in their off-duty pastimes. However, he worked hard to kill this idea, and he worked characteristically in his unspectacular and not particularly obvious way. He tried to interest his friends in the things that interested him—in the history and the glory of France. He arranged impromptu lectures, actually persuading the other private soldiers to come to them, and never appeared to be annoyed when the bugler interrupted him by sounding "Cookhouse" or "Lights Out" and his audience vanished noisily or silently—depending on the occasion—but always swiftly.

He got to know the neighborhood, and took to visiting all the places of historic interest. Later he even persuaded some of his friends to go with him on these excursions.

His reading of history had made him conversant with the seventeenth-century siege of Arras, when "the Great Condé," Prince Louis de Bourbon, who had married Richelieu's niece, and led the dissident party known as the Fronde against the Government during the minority of Louis XIV, fought the army of the Vicomte de Turenne. Now Charles was able to reconstruct the battle in the closest detail, on the banks of the river Scarpe, and use it for one of his lectures.

He often went to the ancient Abbey of Saint-Vaast, where the treasures of the centuries once again revived in him the dreams of past glories and hopes for the future based on the greatness of France. The Arras Museum was also one of his favorite places for spending his time away from the barracks square.

But he was not always intent on bringing a little color into his humdrum existence as an ordinary soldier. Where others went to the cafés to drink, de Gaulle would wander along the Scarpe, thinking out some problem of military science. He was already convinced that war between France and Germany was near to inevitable for the reason that German fever for expansion must lead to a collision between two Powers with growing colonial empires. And he was also convinced that the French Army, as it was constituted and trained at that time, would be ill equipped to stand up to an enemy which had numerical superiority if nothing else.

De Gaulle had seen an airplane only once in his life, but already the idea that the airplane could be of value, even of decisive importance, in war was beginning to take shape in his mind. He discussed the matter with his father at every opportunity, and found the older man in complete agreement with him. Charles even then had some half-formulated idea that he might one day be able to carry troops from place to place by air.

At the end of the year he had not made a great mark on the Army, but the Army had served him well. De Gaulle had learned the thinking and reasoning processes of the ordinary man in the ranks; had noted the little points of irritation which constantly upset equilibrium, and there-fore were damaging to morale. He stored away all these impressions, determined that when he himself became an officer, particularly when he saw active service, he would do his utmost to see that discipline was always tempered with discretion, and that the morale of his men should always be his first consideration. That habit made de Gaulle the natural leader who could rally a defeated nation when there were others who seemed to have a greater right as well as a greater ability.

The day came when de Gaulle made up his pack for the last time in the Ninth Company, had it once more torn to pieces by his sergeant, and went out of that man's life into the classrooms of the Special Military School of Saint-Cyr, where France's infantrymen and cavalrymen received their education in war.

Already he was determined that when he passed out of Saint-Cyr he would ask for a posting back to the 33rd Regiment. Here again he revealed the extraordinary self-confidence he has, for at Saint-Cyr it is necessary to be among the leading graduate cadets to be granted the honor of naming one's posting.

During the two years of his study at Saint-Cyr there was little on the surface to suggest that de Gaulle would ever have the opportunity of naming his regiment. He appeared to be putting in as little work as possible, and, though he was smart on parade and never guilty of deliberately flouting rules and regulations, he was an obvious non-conformist. His love of practical jokes persisted, and he and his great friends Jacques de Sieyes and Alphonse Juin (later to become his Chief of Staff in the Free French Army) were always in the forefront of any mischief that was afoot.

Being at Saint-Cyr meant that de Gaulle was able to get home every weekend, where, after Mass on Sundays, he and his father would discuss the Army and soldiering and the growing threat from Germany. And by now it was becoming evident that the airplane would indeed have some important part to play in military affairs. That and the proper use of mechanically propelled vehicles and of the great firepower provided by the machine gun were the things that de Gaulle spent most time in considering.

He used to lecture his fellow-cadets on these matters, though often he had to admit that their reception of his efforts was no more enthusiastic than had been that of his fellow-soldiers at Arras. But in his lectures de Gaulle saw an opportunity of sizing up his problems and observing and correcting his mistakes. He found that the constant mulling over of a matter gradually brought clarity to his thinking.

He was also developing his writing talent and, under various assumed names, contributing verse and prose to literary reviews. He had a great skill in Greek, and his phenomenal memory made it easy for him to memorize enormous passages of verse.

Charles de Gaulle passed out of Saint-Cyr on October 1, 1912, and to the surprise of many was placed in the first ten of the 700 cadets. When choice of regiment was given him he chose at once the 33rd, and was sent back to Arras as *sous-lieutenant*. Now more than six feet tall, "La Grande Asperge" was the tallest officer in the regiment.

4

A New Theory of War

❧ It was more than a desire to serve as an officer among his old friends which prompted de Gaulle to ask to be posted to the 33rd Regiment of Infantry. Commanding the regiment was a Colonel Philippe Pétain, for whom he had a very great respect. He saw in Pétain, who was later to become a Marshal of France, and then was to fail his country at the crucial moment of German occupation, a man who had gifts of leadership above the ordinary, and also one whose military outlook was almost as revolutionary as his own.

That first posting was to de Gaulle a part of his own developing plan. Observers have affected to see in it the working of fate—certainly it has seemed like that as things have worked out—but de Gaulle would prefer to think that his path crossed that of Pétain so many times because of their mutual liking and respect for each other. That de Gaulle should have at the end condemned his old commander did not in fact mean that his admiration for many of Pétain's qualities had died away. The decision had nothing of personalities about it. De Gaulle condemned a man who, he had decided, had wrought ill for France. In that light no ties of friendship, no ideas of loyalty, have any place.

At the very first at Arras, Pétain was made to know that in his command he had a young officer of striking origi-

nality of thought. It was de Gaulle who was always on
hand when a young officer's services were required. It
was not that he ostentatiously impressed his presence on
his commanders. More often than not they met him per-
forming some original, though not always officially recognized, military exercises. But it was soon very apparent
that here was a young officer whose whole being was
wrapped up in the life of the Army, and Pétain himself
was sufficiently a reformer to observe and to record some of
the novel views of his most junior officer. Pétain liked the
strict discipline of the young man, which was still gener-
ously leavened with sympathy and understanding for the
ordinary soldier. Pétain was amused at first, but later most
impressed, by the way in which de Gaulle met his men and
talked with them on many different subjects—but chiefly
of France and her history and of the French Army and
its glory.

It was almost inevitable, when an officer was required to
take over the training of all intakes of recruits to the 33rd
Regiment, that Pétain selected de Gaulle and followed his
training with the deepest interest. These boys soon came
to know that in Lieutenant Charles de Gaulle they had a
leader of quality such as none of them had ever seen before. The young man got to know every one of his men
personally—his family background and his likes and dis-
likes. On this basis he was able to build a friendship that
could endure under the strains of strict military discipline.
One of his private soldiers of these days says of him, "He
could give you the impression that he thought the world of
you even when he was pronouncing punishment on you."

Pétain also shared de Gaulle's views on the glories of the
France of the past and the value to the soldier of learning
about them through the battles that have been fought on

her soil. Here at Arras, Pétain was as avid a student of the siege, of the military prowess of the Prince de Condé and of Turenne as de Gaulle. And one day Pétain lectured the officers of the regiment on the great battle of Arras in 1654.

The officers sat in silent and respectful lines as Colonel Pétain unfolded stroke by stroke the course of the battle. The Colonel showed the tactical mistakes made by both sides, and particularly by Turenne, despite his eventual victory. In Pétain's view the Prince de Condé had administered a tactical lesson to the royal French Army commanded by the Vicomte de Turenne. Pétain's listeners sat on in respectful silence. All except one. Suddenly from the back of the room came a loud interruption. "But, surely, Colonel, the proof of the tactical skill is in the eventual result. You say that it was correct that Condé, having captured La Ferté, should not have outflanked Hocquincourt. But surely, sir, the answer is that the firepower of Turenne was so great and so well handled that the Prince de Condé was persuaded not to persist in the engagement, and by that means Arras was saved."

There was a momentary gasp of astonishment from the rest of the officers, and de Gaulle reddened with embarrassment at his own audacity. "Stand up, Lieutenant de Gaulle," Pétain ordered. "You have obviously studied your Siege of Arras very thoroughly. I applaud your reading of the lessons of the battle, and we must talk over it again some time."

Colonel Pétain paused for a moment. "The General Staff still have a great belief in the irresistible power of the bayonet," he said when he continued. "But I believe that it is firepower that directs the course of battles to-day, and that the bayonet attack is destined to play a smaller and smaller part in all military strategy in the future."

This was practically in accordance with de Gaulle's own beliefs, though to firepower he was already wishing to add speed and penetration. The commanding officer and the young lieutenant found themselves drawn even closer together after this incident. Repeatedly Pétain found himself sending for the young man to discuss points of military science, and in their off-duty moments they had many animated discussions on the battles of old.

A story is told of the occasion when the 33rd Regiment took part in the celebration of Bastille Day in Arras. On that day there was always a great military parade in the Grande Place. Pétain, mounted on a military charger, took the salute as his men marched past smartly to attention. Lieutenant de Gaulle was at the head of his platoon, but the young officer was surprised by a sudden movement on the part of the Colonel, who rode his horse through the parade to gain the other side of the square.

De Gaulle's men fell into sudden confusion. They missed their step and became hopelessly entangled. While the wits of the crowd laughed and shouted their advice, a flustered de Gaulle strove to gain control again. Then, white-faced, he marched his men back to barracks.

It was an angry Pétain who interviewed his young second lieutenant. "You have disgraced the regiment," he said, "by this slovenly display of marching. You will be confined to barracks for eight days from to-day, and perhaps in that time you will be able to teach your platoon how to halt when on the march."

De Gaulle saluted and went away. But he made no attempt to alter his plans to go home to see his parents that weekend. This was a regular journey for the young officer, and one which his mother and father looked forward to almost as much for the chance it gave of learning the developing facets of his military life as for seeing their son again. Henri de Gaulle, indeed, was showing an absorbing interest in the Army career of his son, and the older man listened to Charles's views in the attitude of pupil rather than erstwhile master. Charles, in the same way, would have done anything to avoid missing his weekends with his family.

So at midday on the Saturday de Gaulle was ready to leave for the station to catch the train to Paris. But the minutes passed, and still there was no sign from the C.O.'s office. It was almost too late when word came that Colonel Pétain had decided that the sentence of confinement to barracks could now be lifted. De Gaulle was out of the gate and his long legs were carrying him towards the train within seconds of receiving the message.

The train was in the station when he arrived. He ran towards it with his suitcase in his hand as it began to move. A passenger in one compartment, seeing him, opened the door for him, and he tumbled in. He looked up to see a civilian looking at him with a smile.

"Well, Lieutenant de Gaulle," said Colonel Pétain, himself on the way to a weekend in Paris, "I see you were all ready to come on leave even though you were still confined to barracks."

"Yes, *mon colonel,*" replied de Gaulle.

"Were you so certain that the sentence would be lifted, then?"

"I knew my colonel too well to think that he would allow an unjust sentence to stand," replied de Gaulle candidly.

Pétain knew that there was nothing of toadying about that remark. By now he had sufficiently gauged the character of his young second lieutenant. They chatted throughout the journey to Paris, and the Colonel gained a vivid impression of what was in de Gaulle's mind so far as the Army was concerned. From that moment Pétain never ceased to watch the young man's progress and keep in touch with his whereabouts.

De Gaulle told his commanding officer that day that he believed the Army of France needed to change drastically its methods and its attitude towards war. He stressed that in his view if and when war came, and he was more than ever certain that it was coming, France would find that its character was completely different from that of any previous war.

"It will not be a war of movement, *mon colonel*," he said. "I believe that the new firepower which the machine gun and the rapid-firing cannon gives to an army will make it essential for the troops of both sides to take to semi-static warfare, in which they will reckon on the sudden sortie to back up the crushing effect of bombardment to force the enemy out of position. I believe that the days of the cavalry are numbered because of this loss of freedom to deploy."

These were views which Pétain himself largely shared. But they were views which were unlikely to be acceptable to the General Staff at that time.

When they returned to barracks after the weekend Pétain set about transforming de Gaulle into an instructor for the regiment. From then on it was Second Lieutenant Charles de Gaulle who was the regimental lecturer in history and in tactics. It was he who gave to the new recruits their first pride of regiment by retelling the great days of the 33rd and of the glorious victories they had gained, and even more glorious defeats they had suffered and survived.

By the time the First World War broke out Pétain had

transformed the 33rd Regiment of Infantry into one of the most highly efficient fighting forces in the French Army. His stock was the very sturdy peasantry and miners of the Tardenois. De Gaulle, promoted lieutenant on October 1, 1913, was three months short of his twenty-fourth birthday when he went to the front.

The 33rd Regiment was flung into action without delay. They formed part of the Second Division of the Fifth Army under General de Lanrezac, described by Sir John French as "the most complete example of the Staff College pedant," and the 33rd were sent in during the first few days of the fighting to hold the advancing Germans before Dinant. When the Germans attacked, the 33rd remained firm against wave after wave of assaults. De Gaulle was always at the head of his men, encouraging and leading them while the town was reduced to rubble around them by the intense artillery bombardment. Here was ample proof of the Pétain and de Gaulle theories of modern warfare, even though the crushing weight of the German attack slowly forced the French and Belgians back.

De Gaulle saw French bayonets thrown into the attack against the German machine guns. The 33rd went into action colors flying and bugles sounding the charge—all very blood-stirring, thought young de Gaulle, as he ran forward at the head of his platoon, but still suicidal and largely wasted valor. He himself was one who fell wounded that day, August 15, 1914, one day before the British Expeditionary Force under Sir John French landed at Boulogne.

On his way to the hospital de Gaulle pondered over the faults of tactics he had seen on the front at Dinant. As the days passed in the hospital and he was able to follow the course of the fighting through the meager communiqués published in the newspapers, he realized how much the French Army was fighting the war on the tactics of past wars. He bitterly criticized Joffre in his conversations with fellow-officers for not altering his tactics to suit the new conditions. De Gaulle was certain that the German plan was to come through at the confluence of the Sambre and the Meuse at Namur. He felt that Namur, though considered virtually impregnable, should be reinforced, and that the General Staff's insistence on the attack through Lorraine to recover the lost provinces of France was foolhardy and merely playing up to national sentiment.

As he lay in bed the German plan became more apparent, and the crushing blow at the Fifth Army put de Lanrezac's troops into full retreat. While the young man prayed from his bed that Joffre would cast off the theories of the past and take matters into his own hands, the miracle occurred, and the French Sixth Army under Maunoury was organized by Galliéni under Joffre and the counter-offensive planned. The first battle of the Marne halted the German tide flowing westward, and soon the French and their British allies were moving back eastward.

De Gaulle was now out of bed again, and he lost no time in applying to report to his regiment. The authorities did not argue this point, for the Fifth Army had been decimated, and with it the 33rd Regiment. De Gaulle arrived back with his regiment to find many of his old friends dead and many others still in the hospital with their wounds. Because he was still not completely recovered from his wound he was made adjutant to Colonel Claudel, the Chief of Staff.

Work at headquarters did not suit the young officer, however, and he obtained permission to take over the col-

lection of information on the enemy movements from the
front line. He was hardly ever out of the trenches from
that time on. He was always ready to take reconnaissance
parties out over the barbed wire and up to the German
lines, listening there to the conversation of the Germans
themselves on many occasions—here his knowledge of
German, learned in school and followed up in military college, was invaluable—and coming back with priceless information on the enemy plans.

As the months dragged past de Gaulle found increasing
evidence of the logic of the talks he had had with Pétain in
the barracks at Arras as to the need for new thinking in
respect of munitions. Though Joffre had saved Paris and
halted the German advance, neither the French nor the
British could advance and take advantage of their tactical
victory because they lacked the necessary guns and ammunition. All this gave the Germans time to regroup and
re-equip.

De Gaulle, with the 33rd Regiment, continued his reconnaissance in the enemy lines. For this he was mentioned in
dispatches on January 20, 1915, in an order of the Second
Division. "Lieutenant Charles de Gaulle has carried out a
series of reconnaissances of the enemy positions under
conditions of the utmost danger, and has brought back
with him information of the greatest value," it read.

But de Gaulle, who by now was becoming almost legend-
ary for bravery in a regiment which had gained a name
throughout the French Army for its valor, was wounded,
for the second time, at Mesnils-les-Hurlus. This time his
wounds kept him out of the line for more than four months.
Then, back again with his regiment, he was promoted captain on September 4, 1915. At this time the regiment was
occupying a place called La Ferme du Choléra, on the

Route 108 close to Berry-au-Bac. One day, leading a patrol into the enemy lines, he was blown up by an enemy mine and seriously wounded.

On October 30, 1915, de Gaulle was given command of the Tenth Company of the 33rd Regiment, and he went with the regiment in February 1916 to the defense of Verdun.

The seriousness of the situation was apparent to the French High Command. Battalion officers were ordered to obtain as much information about the disposition of the enemy and his plans as possible. The commanding officer of the 33rd Regiment chose de Gaulle as his chief reconnaissance officer, and the young man accordingly went out over No Man's Land on several occasions bringing back information of the utmost value.

His commanding officer, Lieutenant-Colonel Boudhors, said of de Gaulle's reconnaissance before Verdun: "I was instructed to send an officer to General Lévy commanding the sector of Douaumont to inform him of the precise position in the light of all the information at our disposal. In view of the gravity of the situation and of the importance attached to the mission, I thought that only Captain de Gaulle was capable of fulfilling it."

There were three lines of French defenses at Verdun, the outer running from Forges and Consenvoye, on the Meuse, to Fresnes, on the Woëvre; the second line ran from Samogneux, through Beaumont, Fosses Wood, and Bezonvaux. Inside this line was a third, running through Bras Douaumont Fort, Hardaumont Wood, Vaux Fort, and Eix.

The 33rd Regiment was at Douaumont, and not immediately engaged when the German assault began on February 21, 1916. In command of the French was General

Pétain, de Gaulle's old commanding officer of the 33rd.

The weight of the German artillery barrage effected some breaches in the French lines, although the defenders, obeying Pétain's vow, "Ils ne passeront pas," held on grimly to their lines. By February 26 Douaumont was in the front line, and it was here that the German Crown Prince launched his supreme assault. The 24th Brandenburger Regiment was selected to lead the advance. Opposing them were the miners and farmers of the 33rd, tense with excitement, because they realized that in their hands that day lay perhaps the fate of France herself.

The spearhead of the German assault, led by the Brandenburger, swept over No Man's Land and into the trenches of the 33rd. The French fought with great gallantry, and no one more bravely than de Gaulle, whose tall figure was easily distinguishable above the smaller blues and greys of the interlocked French and German troops. Time and again the Germans were thrown back; time and again they came on afresh and flooded over the trenches and into the village and redoubt. Victory seemed to be in the German grasp when suddenly over the land from the west swept the fresh reserves which Pétain had kept just for this emergency. Captain de Gaulle rallied his company and led them into the attack with the other companies of the regiment. They swept forward irresistibly, and the German line wavered. Within minutes of the Crown Prince's telegram from his headquarters, "Douaumont, the eastern pillar of the Verdun defenses, is solidly in German hands," the enemy were reeling back.

Again the German troops rallied, and the French advance was halted. The officers of the 33rd Regiment led their men into one more effort. Now it was hand-to-hand fighting, with de Gaulle using his pistol at point-blank range. But suddenly a German lunged forward with his bayonet, and the weapon passed through de Gaulle's thigh and brought him crashing into the mud. And almost at once he was struck on the head by a piece of shrapnel from an exploding shell. A few minutes later he was separated from his men, still fighting in another corner of the field. Night fell, and the battle was halted while both sides regrouped and replenished their supplies.

De Gaulle was unconscious. In any case his leg wound would have prevented him walking. When he recovered consciousness he was being carried through the darkness. There were German voices in his ears, and soon he became aware that these were the members of a patrol returning from reconnaissance in the French lines. "I realized that these men who were now saving my life were those who only a little time before in the hand-to-hand struggle were trying desperately to kill me," he recalled.

As de Gaulle passed into German captivity and out of the War Pétain was issuing a citation:

> Captain de Gaulle, commanding a company which is reputed for its valor, intelligence, and high morale, was, with his regiment, subjected to a bombardment of unprecedented ferocity, which was followed by an assault decimating the battalion and surrounding it on all sides. Captain de Gaulle rallied his men and led them in a furious counterassault and into a hand-to-hand struggle, the only solution that he judged compatible with his military honor. He is an officer without equal in every respect.

The citation carried with it the award of the Cross of Chevalier of the Legion of Honor.

5

The Prisoner of Ingolstadt

❖ From the battlefield of Douaumont de Gaulle was carried to a field dressing station, where his wounds were given a temporary dressing, and he was then taken on to the forward hospital, where German doctors attended to him more thoroughly. He does not remember much of this, as he was often unconscious and unable to grasp what was happening to him. But within a few days he was conscious again, and knew that he was being taken by hospital train back eastward into Germany. Soon he was in the prisoner-of-war camp hospital at Friedberg. There, as his strength came back to him, he began to get restive.

As soon as he was about again he made his first plans to escape from the camp. It was typical of him that it was a solo effort and that everything had to be thought of. But he was acutely conscious that his six feet four inches made him a good target for the German sentries.

De Gaulle was a prisoner who did not mix freely with the rest of the men in the camp. He carried himself with dignity at all times, and he was scrupulously attentive to his appearance, so that he was a credit to the Army of France. He did not show much enthusiasm for the normal occupations of his fellow-prisoners—desperate attempts to fill in the hours of boredom and inaction. To de Gaulle the enforced captivity was a challenge just as much as any other part of his life.

He could speak and read German. But he decided that a fluent knowledge of the language would be invaluable—first because it would make his chances of escape better, second because he was very sure that France and Germany would always be competitors in war or in economics, third because he felt that it was a most profitable way of filling in the weary hours.

But he was an uncooperative prisoner who was most unpopular with both the guards and the commandant of each prison he lived in. At each one—Friedberg, Rosenberg, Szuczyn, Magdeburg, and, finally, Ingolstadt—he made attempts to escape during the two years of his imprisonment. He had every kind of ingenuity, and found it easy to get clear, but each time his great height gave him away by singling him out from the ordinary German soldier and making more apparent the rather amateurish cut of the uniforms he had made for himself.

When the black moods of despair came over him after an abortive attempt to get clear to rejoin his regiment and he received the consequent punishment of solitary confinement, he would turn to his memories of the Greek poets. He found that he could remember thousands of lines, and took to repeating them aloud when in solitary.

Finally he came to the conclusion that his only chance of escape was to tunnel his way to freedom. He chose an accomplice on this occasion, the aviator Roland Garros, and day after day they spent in the confined space of a rock tunnel, chipping away at the rock and with incredible patience and effort moving nearer and nearer to freedom. But before they could strike the open air they were surprised by the guards. De Gaulle, having tried so often to escape, was sent, with Garros, as a punishment to the infamous Fort IX at Ingolstadt, where the recalcitrant prisoners were collected together for greater security.

When de Gaulle came to Ingolstadt he was not in good health. The punishments he had had to undergo as a result of his noncooperative attitude, combined with the poor food, had begun to tell on him. But the reception he received at Ingolstadt helped to revive him somewhat.

Ingolstadt stands on both banks of the Danube, and the forts were on flat land above the river. As he came to the gateway to his prison de Gaulle looked at the date above the gateway. It was to him as if he had been openly insulted, for the figures were 1870.

The fort was sixty feet high, and all round it was a wide but shallow moat. He and his guard waited by the iron door while it was opened from the inside, and then de Gaulle saw in front of him a courtyard which led to a second moat, quite fifty feet wide. The roadway crossing had an iron gate, and a sentry stood guard at it. Beyond was another courtyard, at the end of which he could see a building almost twenty feet high, on top of which was a huge mound of earth in the form of a slope.

As he reached the courtyard his tall figure immediately attracted attention, and more than a hundred prisoners rushed towards him and his guard and, forming into two lines, cheered and shouted, "Verdun! Verdun!" and sang the "Marseillaise" and "On les aura." The guard tried to push them back and presently, as the Frenchmen in the crowd shook de Gaulle's hands and asked him anxiously if he had anything to declare, and said that he should hand it over to prevent it falling into German hands, a very fat and angry commandant came out into the courtyard and began to shout for silence. Immediately he was answered by roars of *"Parle pas, boche!"*

De Gaulle carried himself with his usual dignity, but his heart warmed to the undefeated air of his compatriots. His face broke into one of its rare smiles as he walked slowly forward through the crowd. A German grasped his shoulder and attempted to hurry him forward, but de Gaulle grasped the man's hand and threw it away from him. In the end he was hustled into the commandant's office.

Commandant Hirsch was a flabby, indeterminate man who looked perpetually worried. He informed de Gaulle that he had very bad reports from other camps on his behavior, and he would not tolerate similar indiscipline in Fort IX. "Now salute and go," he ordered.

"You cannot talk to a French officer in that fashion," de Gaulle snapped at him. "I insist that you apologize."

Hirsch's face turned almost purple with his rage. "Get out of the room!" he screamed. "I will see that you are punished for your impudence."

"I will not go until I have received your apology," de Gaulle told him, but two N.C.O.'s hustled him from the room.

They reached their room by an underground passage through more iron doors into the inner courtyards of the fort. The walls were of bare stone, and doors led into the barracks-rooms of the prisoners. Everything was cold and dark, and had the smell of a tomb. The rooms themselves were each a little over fifty feet square, and there six prisoners lived—cooking their food, eating it, and sleeping there.

De Gaulle was slow to settle down. The dreariness of Fort IX, the monotony, and the fact that escape now was almost impossible for once almost crushed his spirit. As usual, he did not make friends easily, despite the excellent souls he found among the French prisoners, who were prouder and more intransigent than any of the mixed crowd of British and Russians. "If I had not remembered

my Greek poetry I think I should have died," he once
told Lieutenant Serreulles, his aide-de-camp of the Second
World War. But gradually he gathered round him a group
of men with tastes similar to his own, so that there were
many opportunities of pleasant conversation. And this and
his own fighting spirit enabled him to beat off his depres-
sion.

The food he found almost uneatable. There was little
enough of it, and what there was was of the poorest quality. Each prisoner had one loaf a day, only a little bigger
than an ordinary bun, one bowl of vegetable soup, one
potato, and sufficient meat to make a moderate plateful
once a week. Whenever a bone was added, the men would
use it for soup time and time again. There was a small
ration of acorn coffee and two lumps of sugar a day. Other
additions to the diet were beans and fish, both in very
small amounts.

His circle of friends included Colonel Tardieu, the senior
Frenchman at the fort, Captain Lelong, Remy Roure,
Berger-Levrault, Catroux, a Russian named Tukhachevsky
—who after the Russian Revolution of 1917 became a general at the age of twenty-seven, a marshal at thirty-five,
and was finally to be executed by his erstwhile comrades—
a Commandant de Goys, La Croix and de Robière, Bellison
and Decugis, all young officers of about his own age.

Fort IX was certainly a more difficult proposition to
escape from than the other prisoner-of-war camps which
had housed de Gaulle, but he was soon actively concerned
in the plans which were constantly being made by all the
prisoners. An Englishman, Lieutenant A. J. Evans, was
the leading light of these escape plans, but he himself
has admitted that it was the French who were the most
ingenious in making clothes and keys and false travel docu-

ments. De Gaulle was a great help in these preliminary preparations.

But very soon he had another interest beyond the actual planning of escape. In fact, he never did make an attempt, as on no occasion did a real opportunity come to him to get away. Instead he set himself to prepare a great and valuable military exercise. One day the idea came to him that it might be useful to analyze the whole course of the war and to pinpoint the mistakes made by each side. In his notebooks he set down the minutest details of bad planning and bad execution. And this extraordinary work, which possibly saved his sanity, was later to set him on the road to world fame as a military writer and a strategist.

Berger-Levrault said of him later, "He is a remarkably gifted officer who will be without doubt, one day, one of the greatest exponents of the military art." Berger-Levrault drew this conclusion following his day-by-day contacts with the prisoner de Gaulle, when he practiced his skill as a strategist and tactician on his usually unwilling fellow-prisoners.

As the old dominant spirit found its resurgence de Gaulle began to arrange lectures for his friends in the camp, lectures on the conduct of war, which he felt might be preferable to lectures on philosophy or even the history of France, with which subjects he could just as easily have filled in the time.

He used to select a particular battle and by means of chalk diagrams on a blackboard demonstrate the faults and the strokes of genius which characterized the movements of the opposing forces.

One day de Gaulle was describing to a group of officers the course of the battle of Champagne of September 25, 1915, in which he had taken part with his 33rd Regiment while at La Ferme du Choléra. He gravely and quietly built up the picture of the assault and its objectives. He showed how the idea was that General de Castelnau should attack with the Fourth Army of General Langle de Cary on a sixteen-mile front from Aubérive to Massiges, so that the German army would be forced back on to the Aisne and enable the French to swing up to cut off the army of the Crown Prince in the Argonne. De Gaulle told how one of the greatest artillery barrages of the war preceded the French assault and, at that moment, glancing at his watch, realized that the half-way stage in the lecture had been reached.

As if he were lecturing in one of the classrooms of the Ecole Militaire, he paused a moment and said, "Ten minutes' rest, gentlemen." A second lieutenant flashed back, "Pencils, stand at ease." There was a roar of laughter from the rest of the room, but de Gaulle showed little sign that it had affected him, save for a wintry smile which was quickly gone.

Ten minutes later he took up the story again. He began by reading out the Order of the Day of General Joffre, which was read to every French soldier on the morning of September 25: "Remember the Marne; conquer or die." His listeners could sense the mounting excitement in him as he told how the waves of French soldiers went forward, bayonets fixed and oblivious of the murderous counterfire of the Germans.

"We had been waiting for this moment for hours," he said, "but as the minutes passed the tension became less easy to bear. We could see the men fidgeting behind us, and we wanted to fidget as well. We looked nervously at our watches, not once, but a score of times, until the moment when H-hour was at hand. Then calmness came back to us until the order to charge was given. Then we were running forward, bending down as if to hide from the machine-gun bullets, which were pouring over us like hail, and the men were following, excited and exultant now, as if they knew that here was history in the making and here was a decisive moment for France."

The lecture came to an end; the voice dropped back into its usual calm, matter-of-fact tones. "That will be all, gentlemen," said Captain de Gaulle, and the meeting broke up.

Sometimes de Gaulle talked to smaller classes of his fellow-prisoners of the works of the great philosophers, even recited his Greek poetry to them, but as the months passed he used his time more and more for a work of the greatest importance—his analysis of the whole course of the war.

He was sitting in his hut one day going through a German newspaper with great care when one of his fellow-prisoners asked him what he was doing.

"I am trying to discover how soon it will be before we win the war," he replied.

"But you'll find only the news of German victories in those papers," his friend said.

"Of course," said de Gaulle, "but if I read these communiqués carefully enough I shall be able to determine what mistakes in tactics the Germans have committed. I feel that I know more or less what the French High Command will do in given circumstances. Therefore I can hazard a guess as to the outcome of the war and its probable finishing date.

"In these bulletins of victory I find the awakening fears of defeat," he added.

These studies made by de Gaulle in Ingolstadt are extraordinary military assessments. Fellow-prisoners who knew of his work have confirmed that long before the news of resounding defeats suffered by the Germans reached them in their prison de Gaulle had worked out their occurrence with a fair degree of accuracy. Thus he foresaw the failure of the great attempt by Nivelle to cut straight through the German center between Soissons and Rheims, a battle which began on April 16, 1917, and went on for eleven days. "We did not have enough strength to carry the day, but the High Command now knows how a breakthrough can be achieved, and the lesson will not be forgotten."

But it was not only German failures that he pinpointed. About those battles in which he had himself taken part his opinions were strong and unshakable. Thus he was not disposed to boast about the great victory of Verdun, but to search through its incidents to discover what were the causes. And he came to the opinion that the French had not been forced out of Verdun because the Germans had lacked the strength to make them give way. That fact, and not the strength of the defensive position, had saved France, he concluded, and from that day his dislike of static defensive positions grew stronger.

Yet, because he was by now convinced that the Allies would win, it was to the disintegration of German military strength that he paid most attention. From the papers that he read he was able to see how the civilian population of Germany was taking a big hand in reducing the will of the armed forces to continue the fight.

The appearance of armored vehicles in warfare intrigued him, and he spent a great deal of his time in pondering on the best ways in which tanks and armored cars could be used offensively to bring about a breakthrough. For hours on end he discussed with Roland

Garros the tactical use of the airplane in warfare, and learned from him the types which were most likely to turn the day.

The young aviator later was transferred to another prison, and from there escaped to get back to France. But he left behind, for de Gaulle to ponder over, the first glimmering of the idea of the war in the air. De Gaulle became fascinated with his schemes for the use of air power, but at this stage he was not thinking so much of the offensive power of the airplane as of its use for reconnaissance and for the carriage of troops and supplies and for bombing behind the enemy lines.

Of tanks he had more positive ideas. He saw in them the means of a massive assault force which would be largely independent of support. It was not until later, of course, that the complete plan for mechanized divisions evolved, but here, on the slopes at Ingolstadt, the first faint stirrings of the idea were coming to him.

His notebooks became filled with what others might have thought was meaningless rubbish. The hastily jotted notes referred to all manner of incidents of the war, at the front and behind the lines. Nothing, he felt, was too small to merit his attention, and nothing was left unread that came into the camp and to his notice.

Thus, though physically he became weaker as the months passed, he became more and more alert mentally, and his imprisonment at Ingolstadt he afterwards came to think was among the most valuable episodes of his life because of the long period of unbroken concentration that it gave him.

6

Defeat of "Méthode a Priori"

❧ It was a very sick man who returned to his home in the Dordogne, where the family were living after the Armistice had been signed. De Gaulle suffered as much from nervous strain at that time as from the effects of poor food and long months of captivity. His imprisonment had been for him one of the most irksome periods of his whole life.

Yet in the few weeks that he spent in the quiet of his home with his parents he gradually was able to draw matters of the greatest value from his years of captivity. He noted down many of the thoughts and conclusions he had come to in the days he had sat solitary on the slopes of the hill above the Danube, and got into clearer perspective all the notes he had made in his prison notebooks. At that moment the idea of setting all this down was only a nebulous thought, but in the talks he had with his father he expounded on the psychological aspects of the German collapse and final defeat.

But he was ready for duty again early in 1919. In May of that year he reported to General Joseph Haller, organizing the Fifth Division of Chasseurs at Sillé-le-Guillaume, and was soon *en route* for Poland and the war with Soviet Russia. General Weygand was then in Poland, reorganizing the Army, and de Gaulle arrived in the Ukraine just in time to take part in the operations of Volhynia at Novo-Georgievsk.

Back in France in November 1919, de Gaulle settled down for a short period to the life of a soldier serving in peacetime. There were visits to his favorite places of history in Paris and to the museums and art galleries that never fail to draw him in his free moments. And it was on one such visit that he met the woman who was to become his wife. In the crowded Salon d'Automne in Paris he was examining the paintings when a friend invited him to the buffet for a cup of tea. The place was crowded, but de Gaulle singled out a tall, slender girl with a mass of straight black hair who smiled at his companion. "Who is the girl?" he asked. His friend answered, "One of my cousins. She's up from the Château de Septfontaines, near Charleville, for the exhibition. Would you like to meet her?"

The two men made their way through the crowd to where Mlle. Yvonne Vendroux was sitting with her parents. Her father was a wealthy industrialist of Calais, who lived at Charleville. It was inevitable that the orchestra in the background was playing "The Destiny Waltz" as de Gaulle was introduced and sat down beside the girl, but at that time the tune was a craze all over the Western world. He balanced his *képi* on his knees and accepted a cup of tea. And then it happened. A cake was offered the young captain. In the crush of people around him the tea tilted, and a stream of hot liquid cascaded over Mlle. Vendroux' dress. De Gaulle sprang to his feet in dismay. The girl, hastily dabbing at her frock, put him at his ease again by laughing gaily. The young man looked into her grey eyes and saw indeed that she was not annoyed, and from that moment he was her devoted admirer. Never since that day have they been long apart, except when official duties have taken de Gaulle away.

The day after the tea incident de Gaulle called at the

hotel where Mlle. Vendroux was staying with her father
and mother to tender his renewed apologies. When the
family went back to their home, the Château de Septfontaines, they left him with an invitation to visit them
there, which he availed himself of within a couple of
weeks.

De Gaulle was tremendously attracted to the girl from
Charleville. Yvonne Vendroux was good-looking rather
than beautiful, but she had a serenity of expression that
often made her almost beautiful. To the young officer her
most attractive characteristic was her ability to keep a
conversation going in the very subjects which interested
him most—outside the military sphere. She proved that
she was well read and that she had been able to marshal
her knowledge so that it could be used to the best advantage.

As the weeks passed and de Gaulle revealed his interest by the number of times he managed to come and
see the girl, they found that they had tastes very much in
common. De Gaulle was to find that Yvonne Vendroux
was almost as facile a writer as he was, and that she could
quote the classics with equal ease.

But even in those days she was shy and retiring. She
was content to allow de Gaulle to monopolize the conversation, but, once embarked on a discussion, she would
argue it tenaciously to a conclusion. Yet never, even
when proved wrong, did she show any resentment.

From the very first de Gaulle knew that he would ask
her to marry him. They were married on April 7, 1920,
just five months after they had first met, and Yvonne de
Gaulle settled down to life in Army quarters, so very different from what she had always been used to.

They lived unpretentiously, and made it a rule to keep

within their Army pay. This habit of frugality has remained
with them all their lives. Yvonne de Gaulle very soon revealed that she had no interest in fashion, never wanting
more than a couple of dresses and always these were of a
quiet, sober design. They made their home life happy by
a careful selection of friends of similar tastes, and the de
Gaulle home was soon famous for its sparkling conversation.

De Gaulle returned to Poland for military service. He
was in time to take part in the defense of Warsaw under
the orders of Weygand, who opposed the Russian armies
commanded by General Tukhachevsky, at twenty-seven
the youngest general in any major Army in the world. For
this de Gaulle received a Mention in Dispatches from
Weygand. This brought him to the notice of Marshal
Joseph Pilsudski, who, on the recommendation of General
Stanislas Haller, Chief of Staff and cousin of Joseph Haller,
offered de Gaulle the post of lecturer in military tactics at
the new Military School at Rembertov, just outside Warsaw.

It was in the Polish Military School that Captain de
Gaulle began to develop his theory of armored warfare
which he had first sketched out in the prison camp at
Ingolstadt. There has since been considerable argument
as to who first thought of mechanized warfare as practiced
by the German Army in 1940. General Fuller of Britain,
the British military critic Liddell Hart, the Austrian General Eimensberger, the German General von Seeckt, all
have their supporters. De Gaulle himself was certainly
not the first to publish his views, but there can be little
doubt that a great many French military specialists of all
ranks were well aware of his ideas within a short time of
the Armistice of 1918. He was outlining mechanized opera-

tions while still on service in Poland in 1920, and the physical make-up of the German Panzer Division was exactly on the de Gaulle plan. The originality of de Gaulle's ideas could have less than proper expression while he was a captain in the line in Poland, but even so it did not pass unnoticed by the Polish General Staff. General Stanislas Haller was of the opinion that his young officer's handling of mixed units of infantry and tanks under a small air cover was as brilliant as anything he had ever seen. He singled out de Gaulle as a man who would one day be a great tactician, and, more than that, as a man who would lead his country in battle. This opinion was strengthened by de Gaulle's work in the Polish Military School.

While still a lecturer there he received an urgent summons back to France to take over the post of Professor of Military History at Saint-Cyr. The order came from the French Ministry of War, and Colonel Mercier, de Gaulle's commanding officer during the Polish fighting, who brought the summons, said that there could be no question of his not accepting. De Gaulle, though the offer sent a thrill of anticipation through him, was in many ways sorry that he would leave Rembertov so soon after setting his theories into motion there. He returned to France with the Cross of St. Wenceslas as recognition of his services.

Saint-Cyr seemed to him not to have changed in the slightest. As he walked the well-remembered corridors and looked in at the lecture rooms the young professor imagined them again peopled with the friends of his youth. He was a brilliant lecturer, who made his course one that few of his students would have missed. At the same time he himself was studying for entry into the Ecole Supérieure de Guerre, the French Staff College. He passed the examination at the first attempt in November 1922,

at the time of his thirty-second birthday. And immediately
the College realized that they had with them a man of
revolutionary ideas who would not be held down by
tradition even if he himself was normally a slave to it.

De Gaulle set himself immediately to expound his new
theories of war. He was convinced that the failure of the
French military system was that it always taught on the
basis of the lessons of the war which had gone before. The
accepted theory of this year that one should establish a
fixed front and on that employ every means of firepower
and defense was impossible and dangerous in his eyes.
This "méthode a priori," as it was called, was the favorite
theory of General Moyrand, the Commandant of the
Staff College. De Gaulle denounced it roundly and openly,
to the anger and dismay of the General and his staff. De
Gaulle argued that there could never be universal systems
of warfare which would suit all conditions, but only
situations created by circumstances and personalities. "You
cannot be sure that you can choose your own positions
from which to fight," he said. "You cannot be sure of a
vast field of fire from which you can direct the most
powerful barrage on the enemy. You must suit your plan
to the circumstances of the situation and to the personalities at your disposal, because you must never think
that your enemy will be less skillful than yourself and will
not refuse to fall into the trap of your prepared positions."

He saw, as clearly as he had seen in the days before the
First World War, that trench warfare was being made
inevitable by the tremendous increase in firepower brought
by machine and rapid-firing field guns, that now, with the
great mobility provided by the tank and the lorry, static
warfare was a thing of the past.

This revolt against accepted theories made de Gaulle the

most unpopular member of his course. Moyrand was
furious that his theories should be so openly flouted whenever they were voiced. So certain was he that he was right
that at the end of the course, when the usual field exercises
were held on the theories that had been taught in the
preceding years, he gave to de Gaulle the command of
Blue Force, while he himself commanded Red Force.

The exercises were carried out near Grenoble, in South-
ern France, in the foothills of the Alps. De Gaulle gathered
his forces about him and reconnoitered the positions. Then,
without taking into account his belief that Moyrand would
adopt his "méthode a priori" in this instance, he proceeded
to do battle in the new style according to the circumstances
of the moment and the men and equipment at his disposal.
In fact, his troops ran up against a fixed line of prepared
positions, which de Gaulle was able to infiltrate and out-
flank with the greatest of ease on account of his mobility.
The senior inspecting officers present were embarrassed for
Moyrand, who, while he could do nothing but admit the
serious reverse he had suffered, was still of the opinion that
luck had favored the young commander of Blue Force.

De Gaulle was punished for his temerity in conducting
an exercise in direct contradiction of all he had been taught
at the Staff College. He was, in fact, demoted, and might
have suffered permanent eclipse in the French Army if
the incident had not reached the ears of his old friend and
commander, Marshal Pétain, then French Chief of Staff.
Pétain came to the Staff College, listened to the facts, then
said, "De Gaulle is right." He sent for de Gaulle. "I hear
you have brought off a resounding defeat of the army of
General Moyrand, Captain de Gaulle. I want you to prepare me a report on the whole conduct of the engagement,
with a full explanation of your reasons for employing every

type of tactics. Take a fortnight over it if you like, but make it thorough."

The report Pétain received from the young student at the Staff College he often described as one of great brilliance. It demonstrated without any doubt the whole fallacy of the "méthode a priori," and revealed that a new theory had arrived. Pétain was so impressed that he sent de Gaulle back to the Ecole Supérieure de Guerre as an instructor in military theory and the functions of a commanding officer. Pétain himself drove to the College to listen to the first lecture, shook de Gaulle warmly by the hand at its finish, and said to one of his close advisers at the War Office, "We have found a brilliant tactician who will go far in the Army."

At the end of his term at the Staff College de Gaulle was appointed to the General Staff by Pétain, until the Marshal himself was succeeded as Commander-in-Chief by Weygand. As soon as this happened de Gaulle, still the active and vociferous proponent of the theory of maneuver, as distinct from that of passive defense, was transferred to the General Staff of the Army of the Rhine. It was 1924 and still in Paris the traditional theories of "méthode a priori" held sway. Pétain himself, although impressed by de Gaulle's obvious development of a better method, had done nothing to make it a substitute, and Weygand was firmly committed to the old theories.

Yvonne de Gaulle packed up once more and went with her husband into Germany and temporary quarters at Mayence. There de Gaulle was able not only to observe the new spirit of belligerence among the German people, but also to record at last his impressions of the German leaders on the lines of his studies in the prison camp of Fort IX. In his first book, *La Discorde chez l'ennemi*, he set himself to analyze the causes of the defeat of Germany in the war, and revealed himself as a writer of French of great distinction. Here already was the style, perhaps modelled on that of Chateaubriand, that has caused de Gaulle to be described as one of the few living men who can write French that is at the same time lucid and rhythmical. "He writes French as if it were Latin," some one said in an attempt to explain the beauty of his style.

In *La Discorde chez l'ennemi* de Gaulle dealt with the psychological, political, military, and moral causes of the German defeat. Though he traced the history of the defeat —the disobedience of General von Kluck, which brought about his defeats on the Marne and the Aisne and his consequent retirement from the Army; the opening of the submarine war by Tirpitz; the intrigues of Ludendorff, which brought about the resignation of Chancellor Bethmann-Hollweg in July 1917; and the gradual disorganization of the German people in face of repeated reverses—he went much further.

De Gaulle recognized the difficulties of reconciling the views of politicians and military leaders in time of war. But he insisted that the soldier must always remain subordinate to the politician, even though the time might come when the mere glorification of material gain would pass away and military service would be a more honorable career than ever before. "But an honor is not a right," he insisted, as he drew attention to the fact that the German generals of the war looked on themselves almost as demigods, who were defeated because of the feebleness of Wilhelm II and the weakness of the political leaders.

But de Gaulle's fiercest attack was on the immoderation of the German people, and particularly of their leaders. He pointed out that the leaders of Germany had all sub-

scribed to the theories of the new Master Race propounded
by Nietzsche, which in following its own glorification is
convinced that it is serving the general interest, regarding
the masses as contemptible, and will not stop in face of
the suffering of humanity.

De Gaulle's was a powerful indictment of the German
people of the day, and he attached to it an appraisal of the
French character in the form of an allegory. "In the French
garden," he said,

> each tree does not seek to suffocate the others with its shade;
> the flower beds are laid in geometric lines; the fountain does not
> aspire to be a waterfall; the statues do not force themselves on
> one's attention to draw admiration. A noble melancholy reveals
> itself at times. Perhaps it comes from the belief that every isolated
> element should be able to shine on its own; but that has weak-
> ened the whole.

La Discorde chez l'ennemi was sufficiently arresting to
make Frenchmen take notice of him where they had perhaps not known him before, and it had a big sale in
Germany.

De Gaulle had looked back over the past and had
analyzed the causes of events which were common knowledge. He risked having the knowing ones declare, "Well,
we knew all that before," when, in fact, he was opening the
eyes of his own countrymen, and of any others who read
his book, to a new appraisal of the German character, and
of the French character too.

One man at least took particular notice of *La Discorde
chez l'ennemi*. Pétain wrote to the publisher of the book:
"Frenchmen would do well to listen to him with care, for
the day will come when France will call for him in
gratitude."

7

The Youthful Strategist

❧ A summons came to de Gaulle late in 1925 to report to Pétain at the office of Vice-President of the War Council in 4 bis Boulevard des Invalides, Paris. There, as aide-de-camp to Pétain, the young officer was set to write a history of the French Army. These historical notes were later to be incorporated in his book *France and Her Army*.

His new job was writing history. His pictures of First World War fighting are especially vivid. Here, of course, he was often describing his own experiences. He told how, before the infantry attack, the men wait for the signal to go over the top, and, as the minutes pass, their nervous tension increases. He used cleverly the idea of the break of dawn, and how, with the coming of the light, the thoughts of men at war turn to whether they will ever see nightfall again. They shiver in the cold of the dawn, and look out over the parapet of the trench for any sign of the enemy or to gauge what effect their own artillery bombardment is having. They look repeatedly at watches, and also at their officers. The officers themselves try to give the appearance of being calm as they give their last-minute instructions.

In one sentence de Gaulle revealed much of his beliefs about Army discipline. He wrote: "As the moment for the attack arrives the ties of discipline tighten for all."

He described also an assault by the enemy, the effect of the tremendous barrage which shatters the trenches and the dugouts and sends the infantrymen, stunned and nerveless, into the bottom of the trench, where living lie down beside the dead. Then, in the smoke and dust of exploding shells, they see the enemy infantry and open fire with machine guns and mortars. Soon the enemy is firing directly into the trenches, and one by one the defenders are wiped out. But they have done their job: they have gained time for reserves to be brought up.

Of these things de Gaulle wrote with pride, but with the object of showing the futility of such tactics in the new world of machines.

De Gaulle wrote of other things at his office in the Boulevard des Invalides. On December 1, 1925, the *French Military Review* published an article by him entitled "The Historic Role of French Fortresses." It was an assignment given him by the Defense Council, which had prepared a plan for the fortification of the region along France's frontier with Germany—the Maginot Line. De Gaulle's description of the northeastern frontier of France was that it is

> a terrible breach which joins to German soil the strategic valleys of the Seine and the Loire, with both the mountains and the rivers hindering defense and helping the invaders by providing a great many routes of penetration: the valleys of the Meuse, the Sambre, the Escaut, the Scarpe, and the Lys, down which not only the rivers but the roads and the railways all seem designed to help an invading army.

The idea of static defense was not one that appealed to de Gaulle, yet he had always seen the vital necessity of producing a plan which would guard these most vulnerable areas of France. He felt that the fortification of these areas was the duty of the Government, but that the plan of operations which would utilize the advantage such fortifications would give the defenders was one for the military command. Thus, as he called on the teachings of his ancestor, Maillot, the pupil of the great Vauban, de Gaulle supported fortifications only in so far as they hampered the mobility of invaders, while giving license to the defender to attack and to infiltrate.

Among military men the article was hailed as something of a triumph. In France generally there was little public reaction, as was to be expected. De Gaulle followed up his article with a series of lectures at l'Ecole Supérieure de Guerre on the subject of "The Art of War and the Commander." Pétain presided, and once more repeated his opinion: "Listen with care to Captain de Gaulle, gentlemen, because one day all France will have occasion to be grateful to him for his foresight."

These lectures were classic expositions of military science, which impressed his audience to such a degree that they were repeated by de Gaulle at the Sorbonne for the benefit of students, Members of Parliament, and public figures.

His call for the employment by France of all the modern technical advances of military science—the tank, the armored car, the airplane, and mobile artillery weapons —was listened to with interest, but brought little active support.

Among the most attentive readers of "The Historic Role of French Fortresses," and one who also listened to the lectures, was Paul Painlevé, the French War Minister, who himself had once been a Professor of Mathematics at the Sorbonne. With André Maginot, Painlevé embarked on the fortification of the northeast frontier of France, the

Maginot Line, which, based on the purely defensive role
of the French Army in previous wars, was intended to keep
out any enemy who dared to pour through the traditional
invasion gaps into France. But Maginot and Painlevé made
no attempt to persuade the Belgians that the Line should
be carried through to the sea.

De Gaulle could not bring himself to support the
Maginot Line as a military policy. His mentor, Pétain, on
the other hand, was now a warm supporter of the project.
It was perhaps inevitable, therefore, that the Marshal and
his assistant should come into direct opposition in the
matter, and that the distinguished supporter of the
"méthode a priori" should come increasingly into argument with the inventor of the new method of movement
and infiltration. In the end, in the spring of 1927, de Gaulle
packed his bags once more and went back to active service
as commandant of the 19th Battalion of Chasseurs à pied
at Trier, in the Rhineland, still occupied by the French.
There, once more, Yvonne de Gaulle set up house and
organized life as the wife of an officer on active duty in a
garrison town.

In the background she helped her husband in his social
work with the men, and the couple gathered about them
a small circle of close friends. But, as in all other places in
which they have served in the Army, she very rarely appeared in public, and was never in the limelight.

Once he had got to know all his men, de Gaulle set
about his training schedule by trying to ensure that they
had most of their working time taken up by actual
maneuvers, and spent as little time as possible on meaningless barracks-square drills and fatigues. His view was
that a soldier does not become bored if he is kept busy
at soldiering. It is only when domestic fatigues are forced

on him day after day that he loses interest, discipline, and smartness.

Though there was little opportunity for de Gaulle to distinguish himself in the comparative backwater of the Rhine Army, his unit became one of the smartest in that army, and his men, all of whom were devoted to him, were trained to an extraordinary efficiency in the science of movement. After an inspection by General Matter, Director of Infantry, the General reported to the War Office in Paris: "I see in de Gaulle a future Commander-in-Chief of the French Army."

De Gaulle was not all the time occupied in training his men, however. He was giving a great deal of thought to the problems of a stirring Germany. He wrote at that time to Lucien Nachin, now a publisher, that the days of the Army of the Rhine were numbered. "I am convinced that the Anschluss is approaching, and that Germany is growing in strength and determination; that she will make claims on the territory of Poland and will reclaim from France the province of Alsace-Lorraine."

He was certain also that the resurgence of Germany presented the world with a danger of world war. His letters many times mentioned the inevitability of world war once Germany began to expand.

But he was not concerned only with the dangers of a new and militant Germany. Another danger gave him matter for thought. He watched reports of the conditions of life inside Soviet Russia, and studied the means by which the Soviets were propagating their Communism. He felt sure that their ultimate aim was the conquest of the world by insidious infiltration. Yet he was not anti-Communist—in fact, he has sometimes been said to have a liking for the better points of Communist ideology. But now he was calling on his memory of all the conversations he had had with Tukhachevsky in Ingolstadt.

In order that he might study the problems of France in Asia Minor, de Gaulle applied for a posting to the Lebanon, and was appointed to the General Staff in Beirut. From 1930 to 1932 he visited successively Damascus, Aleppo, and Baghdad, staying for short periods in each. He also paid visits to Palestine and Egypt. It was natural to his character that he should make a careful study of Islamic problems, and he soon came to the conclusion that for France there were only two possible courses of action —to stay as rulers or to get out. He realized that the Arab could not be changed and could not be wooed. He put on record his opinion that only one Frenchman really understood the situation and could control it for France— Colonel Catroux, "Le Roi Catroux," as he was called, his old comrade in the prison camp at Ingolstadt, and since that time an officer who had seen considerable service in the Middle East. But de Gaulle added bitterly, "It is just because he is such an expert on the problems of the Lebanon and Syria that he has been sent away from here." Years later de Gaulle was to use Catroux in the Middle East at a time crucial to France.

Back in France in 1932, de Gaulle set himself to analyze the conclusions he had reached over the whole range of his foreign experiences. He felt that France was lagging in her development of her natural resources and her internal economy. He felt that it was essential that the whole power of the French Empire could be mobilized for the defense of the country. He set himself to write a personal testimony which finally showed that he had broken with the old system of defense which his superiors still clung to with blind faith. His book, *Le Fil de l'épée* (often wrongly called *Au Fil de l'épée*), which means putting an edge on the sword, was an expression of his faith. He dedicated the book to Pétain; his friend Berger-Levrault was the publisher.

In the beginning of the book de Gaulle dealt with the problems which the act of war raises because it involves the taking of human life. He argued that these problems could be resolved only by a combination of instinct and intelligence. There was no sure guide to behavior in war. He went on to discuss the necessity for men of character to be placed at the head of affairs, in order that great problems could be met by great resolution. Without a strong character, he said, Alexander the Great would not have conquered Asia. Galileo overcame difficulties to demonstrate the movement of the earth, and Columbus had to show the greatest depths of character before he discovered America. Richelieu would never have restored the authority of Louis XIII without strong character, nor Nicholas Boileau, the seventeenth-century poet and critic, established the rules of classical taste. Without character, which enabled him to act on his own, Napoleon would never have founded the Empire, nor would de Lesseps have driven through the Suez Canal in face of all the difficulties and discouragements. Bismarck would never have attempted to achieve the unity of the German peoples, and Clemenceau would never have saved France, if either had listened to prudent counsels and timid advice.

Moreover, he argued that often for the man of character and action it is necessary to show disregard of discipline: in his youth at school and in the Army he had often shown restiveness to unnecessary discipline. De Gaulle cited as examples of this disregard of orders the manner in which his own General Lanrezac had saved the French Army after Charleroi in the First World War by breaking off the action in spite of the orders he received. He drew attention to Marshal Lyautey, who kept all Morocco in 1914 against the instructions of his superiors, and he also recalled the story told after the battle of Jutland, when Admiral Fisher, hearing the report of Admiral Jellicoe on the failure of the British Fleet to destroy the German Fleet, wrote: "He [Jellicoe] has all the qualities of Nelson save one; he does not know how to disobey." These also were lessons de Gaulle had learned which he used and has continued to use in his own life, and which were to be used by his supporters in Algiers in 1958.

He attacked the doctrine of the "méthode a priori" once more, and laid at its door all the disasters of the war of 1870. He drew an adverse comparison between the passive resistance of the military chiefs who believed in the defensive and the brilliant campaigns of Napoleon.

He turned also to the question of the politicians as they came into contact with the soldier, and here, once again, he showed how much he disliked the theories of Nietzsche about the Master Race. This work, *The Edge of the Sword,* was an important exposition of de Gaulle's own beliefs, which have a bearing on his recent actions. He reiterated that force must be used only on the side of justice. To him authority and liberty were absolutely inseparable. He believed that though the absolutely despotic state was incapable of existing for long, so was the state based entirely on complete liberty. To him liberty which set itself against all authority was incapable of existing without that authority.

De Gaulle confessed that he did not like arms, which have always been the instruments of barbarism. "Arms stir up in the heart the mud of the worst instincts," he said. He has always had a strong aversion to the taking of human life. Yet "the deeds, the courage, the devotion, the loftiness of soul, of men in battle enables them to reach the summits and to enrich the sum of human morals," he wrote.

From this philosophy about man at war—the philosophy of command—de Gaulle came to the conclusion that in the modern world government—that is, government by the political representatives of the people—and the military must collaborate to ensure equilibrium in the state.

The Edge of the Sword attracted a great deal of attention. It has since always been regarded as de Gaulle's most striking declaration of his faith and beliefs. In its pages the character of the man is revealed time and again, and in all its many sides. His scholarship is shown in the turn of phrase, the selection of adjectives, the breadth of example. His study of philosophy is also revealed here. The man of religion and of brotherhood shines out from the pages of his book. There also are the lonely man and the man who would treasure friends. Above all de Gaulle demonstrated in *The Edge of the Sword* that he was a wise man. But, unfortunately, in 1932 there were all too few in France to look and to listen and understand.

He followed his book up on May 10, 1933, with an article in The Political and Parliamentary Review, which showed more clearly the lines on which his military thoughts were proceeding. He declared then that the necessity for France to be protected, the demands of military techniques and international developments, made it essential for her to accept a profound military reform.

De Gaulle was, in fact, in process of evolving his own revolutionary theory. The idea came to him as much from a philosophical study of the world about him as from a definite search for something new in war. The advance of the machine age, the mechanization of almost every industrial process, convinced him that war must be similarly mechanized. Production-line methods in the factory, the nonstop moving forward of the article being manufactured, were pointers to what military men would call for and develop in future wars, he was now convinced. Here was the germ of the idea for the mechanized division and army which, once on the move, would never stop until the end of the particular engagement was reached.

8

Birth of the Armored Division

❦ 1932 marked a stage in de Gaulle's military career which was of more significance than anything he had previously undertaken. He was appointed Secretary-General of the Council for National Defense. Pétain and Weygand were his sponsors for this post, which brought de Gaulle in close contact with the political leaders of France and with military planning on a national scale.

What he learned and what he saw discouraged him at first. Nowhere in France apparently was there any realization that Germany had fired new strength and new determination in the ashes of her defeat. While France had grown weaker her old enemy had, by the sheer necessities of defeat and disaster, come out of those trials stronger than ever. That was something that de Gaulle had warned of in his *Discorde chez l'ennemi.*

In his new job he learned everything about the defenses of France, the planning for defense, and the methods to be adopted in face of attack. The defense plan was almost entirely static, and therefore in his view dangerously inadequate in face of the threatened war of movement.

He was convinced that he knew the type of army that the aggressor would throw into battle. He had now been promoted to lieutenant-colonel and he felt that his views might be given some attention by his superiors. There was

hardly a waking moment of his life when he was not
thinking and talking of the needs of France and of the type
of army which might ensure her safety. He lived at the
time with his wife at the Hôtel Lutétia in the Boulevard
Raspail, a quiet and modest establishment which perfectly
suited their needs and temperament. Yvonne de Gaulle,
as always, devoted her whole time and energies to her
husband and her son and two daughters. She was rarely
seen in public even at the official receptions that her
husband had to attend.

De Gaulle himself was as active socially as he had ever
been. He had become convinced that in order to get his
ideas listened to he must make friends with those holding
like views. It was not sufficient occasionally to write an
article for some review with a limited circulation, or even
a book, which would have ephemeral success and then
be forgotten.

He had, indeed, become friendly with one man at least
who shared his alarm over the state of French defenses.
This was a retired soldier, Lieutenant-Colonel Emile
Mayer, who had been at school with Joffre and at the
Ecole Polytechnique with Foch. Moreover, Mayer had
been a friend of Hippolyte Taine, the French historian and
philosopher, one of de Gaulle's favorite authors. That
provided a different topic of conversation when, very occasionally, de Gaulle tired of military talk.

Between de Gaulle and Mayer there soon developed the
closest friendship. They met every Monday evening at the
Brasserie Dumesnil, at the corner of the rue de Rennes,
opposite the Gare Montparnasse. Mayer's knowledge of
Joffre and Foch made him an invaluable source of information to de Gaulle, whose study of the great soldiers had
been carried out at a distance. They would discuss Joffre's

theories, his triumphs and his disasters, his experiences as Chief Technical Adviser to the Allied Forces in the First World War, and how his theories fitted the present time. They talked of Foch, a man very much after de Gaulle's own heart, with his belief in the offensive. Indeed, a favorite quotation of de Gaulle at that time was Foch's memorable and laconic message to General Headquarters when his Ninth Army had been terribly battered by the Germans in the first battle of the Marne on September 8, 1914. "My center is giving away, my right is falling back, the situation is excellent. I shall attack," Foch declared. This was fully in accord with de Gaulle's belief that attack is always the best defense.

Soon the two men were joined by others of like views and aims: Mayer's son-in-law was M. Grünebaum-Ballin, who knew every one who was anyone in France, and was therefore in a splendid position to lay before the important people the views of the earnest Secretary-General of the Council for Defense. There was Berger-Levrault, an old friend of de Gaulle's of his days in the 33rd Regiment, who had become a publisher and had given de Gaulle's own books to the world. (He is still de Gaulle's publisher from his office in the Boulevard Saint-Germain.) There were many others, some merely passing visitors, who stopped by to listen to sparkling conversation and intriguing expositions of military science and planning.

De Gaulle talked mechanization and movement all the time. In his mind was developing the clearest picture of the army of the future, in which mobility and firepower were blended to such a degree of flexibility that no sudden reversal of fortune in battle would throw the force completely out of its offensive stride. For the doctrine of de Gaulle was "Offense. Always attack."

He was at that time working on the details of the French plan for a supranational army to be administered through the League of Nations, which was to be placed before the Assembly in Geneva. But at the same time he was uneasily aware that the chances of such a revolutionary idea being adopted were small. He was even more disturbed at the sad state of the French military organization. Therefore he continued to work on his new theories of a small force of specialists equipped with the latest in tracked vehicles and capable of tremendous firepower and mobility.

But even as de Gaulle was working officially to bring into being a mechanized force, so Pétain was continuing his almost unbelievable campaign against such an army. Before the Senatorial Commission on the Army on March 7, 1934, the Marshal declared: "What would be the use of a great mass of tanks arriving in the region of Paris? Lorry-borne troops and a few armored cars would be enough to checkmate an invasion by the German armored corps."

In his typically methodical way de Gaulle went into the greatest detail in his appreciation of the situation as he saw it. All the ideas about the use of aircraft and mechanically propelled vehicles which he had had since his youth, and on which he had never ceased to work throughout his Army career, were assembled and put into proper place. He studied the make-up of the armies of the past, both French and foreign, dissected them down through their divisions and brigades and regiments. He went back as far as the armies of Napoleon Bonaparte for his comparisons, and contrasted the firepower of the ancient muzzle-loader muskets and the modern machine guns. He compared the meager information that he had himself been able to bring back from his reconnaissances of the First World War with what one low-flying reconnaissance aircraft could now bring back from a single swift flight.

He felt that war, because it had become so much more complicated than it was when his ancestor Jean de Gaulle was fighting against the English at Agincourt, required much more thought in the planning of the army if the machine was not to become completely unwieldy. He realized that, though it was true that in these times it was not the fighting soldier who was most important in battle, but the equipment and the machines at his disposal, a superabundance of these aids to greater firepower and mobility could in fact be a drag on, and a danger to, the man.

De Gaulle reckoned that the modern infantryman needed to use fifteen different weapons, the artilleryman had sixty-eight at his disposal, and the engineers must handle sixteen different types of mechanical equipment. There must also be in close attendance on the army the corps of supply—the ammunition and spare-parts supply-lines—all very intricate, and growing more intricate with every new invention. He worked on the problems of ensuring that the army in rapid movement could be supplied with sufficient ammunition for its multiplicity of weapons and the many thousands of spare parts needed to keep its mechanical equipment moving and efficient.

He studied the needs of the new-style signal systems of the army—the field-telephone network for closed-circuit messages and the many different radio aids to rapid communication. He analyzed the minimum needs of the army in the subject of range- and direction-finding equipment, photographic reconnaissance, maps and map interpretation, compasses, the use of camouflage, and its carriage and disposal. He studied the problems of possible gas at-

tacks and the use of even more unethical methods of warfare, and how such tactics could be combated.

De Gaulle's next stage of his military appraisal was to
analyze what was required of the modern soldier. It was,
of course, obvious to him—the same could not be said of
some other commanders—that the infantryman of Napoleon's time would be out of his depth in the modern
army, and that regimental drill of the type still carried
out on France's barracks squares was of no value in preparing a man for what he would have to face in actual
battle. But these were the views that had brought official
strictures on the young subaltern de Gaulle when he first
joined the 33rd Regiment at Arras. Though he had
adapted and advanced his views to the changing patterns
of warfare, he had not radically altered them.

Now he realized that the need to have a highly trained
technician as a soldier meant that the numbers who could
be trained would be reduced. And from this he proceeded
naturally to the organization of the new-style fighting division of the army of the future. Based on mobility, he
himself envisaged that it would move entirely in tracked
vehicles.

De Gaulle proceeded to organize his army, on paper, on
the basis of six divisions of the new mobile type. In each
division he placed one armored brigade equipped with
fast tanks and with 150 medium-caliber guns, 400 light
guns, and 600 machine guns. This brigade was formed of
two tank regiments, one in heavy and one in medium
tanks, and a reconnaissance regiment in very fast armored
cars. His infantry brigade he organized into two regiments
of foot and a battalion of scouts, and the equipment consisted of 50 guns of field caliber, 60 anti-tank guns, and
600 machine guns. Also de Gaulle planned to have two

regiments of artillery with his division, one with heavy
field guns designed to operate at short range and the other
with light field guns of much longer range. To these he
added an anti-aircraft regiment for protection of the
whole division, where possible, from aerial attack.

The idea of the tactical air force under the direct order
of the divisional commander had already come to de
Gaulle, and he provided for a unit of several squadrons—
the exact number he felt would be dictated by the operations assigned to the division—which would move everywhere with the division and utilize airfields within the
division's sphere of operations.

With incredible attention to detail, de Gaulle went into
the new role of camouflage in modern warfare. He realized that if mobility and firepower were to be the main
weapons of attack surprise was every bit as important.
The lightning blow depended on catching the enemy un-
awares. Therefore the art of camouflage must be studied
by every soldier, and there must be specialized camouflage units attached to every division. He visualized these
units engaged on producing false columns of vehicles,
false vehicles and aircraft, false fortifications and earth-
works, misleading lights and noises of movement, false
radio and light signal messages. How important were
these ideas to prove in the war of 1939-45, when both sides
brought the element of camouflage and misleading information to a fine art!

In the Brasserie Dumesnil this new army took shape
over the tables at which the friends sipped their coffees or
their *apéritifs*. The little group grew larger. Remy Roure,
the old friend of de Gaulle in the days of captivity, used to
take part in the discussions. General Baratier, General
Duval, Pierre Bourget, Le Cour Grandemaison, Philip

Serre, and Charles Giron all from time to time gave the young Colonel de Gaulle their interest and support.

In his spare time de Gaulle was at work on a book which would explain his theories and advance his views. Published in May 1934, his *L'Armée de métier* was an immediate success, and was later published in English under the title *The Army of the Future*. In its pages he set out the theories he had propounded at the Dumesnil meetings. His book had a profound effect on many military leaders in a number of countries, but not least in Germany, where his views were already given the utmost weight owing to his penetrating analysis in *La Discorde chez l'ennemi*.

L'Armée de métier was a complete appraisal of the military situation as it affected France. It covered the widest ground. De Gaulle warned those who felt that the mere possession of mountain ranges along the borders gave consequent protection. True, the forbidding peaks and slopes of the Pyrenees, the Alps, the Jura, and the Vosges appeared to offer splendid opportunities for delaying tactics on a fast-moving enemy, particularly because of the wild valleys of the great river systems of the Garonne, Rhône, and Meuse. But there were gaps—particularly the Belfort Gap—and the whole frontier with Belgium still remained unfortified.

De Gaulle named five French rivers as being the danger words for France—Sambre, Meuse, Aisne, Oise, and Marne. Though these are the traditional battlegrounds of the French, they were to assume an even more disastrous importance than formerly in the war he was now warning against. "Along these rivers, it is easy going to the heart of France and to Paris," he wrote in *L'Armée de métier*.

His was the appreciation of a general. He added to that

a knowledge of history and an understanding of the German mind, for it was always the Germans he had in his mind as the potential enemy. The benefits of an attack through Belgium towards France had always been obvious to military men of most countries. So had the fact that almost all the west-to-east railways passed across the French frontier to the north of Thionville, close to the Saar and to Luxembourg.

At this period of his life de Gaulle felt that there was a natural and incurable enmity between the Gauls and the Teutons. He felt that only when both sides were exhausted by war or were in common danger did they ever draw close together and appear to give promise of friendship.

His study of the German mind, which enabled him to see so clearly the steps that would be taken when war finally came, may well have been the first real attempt at the psychological approach to war, which only five years later was to assume the greatest importance. Although de Gaulle did not turn to astrology to determine what would be the next move of his adversary, he was able to forecast it by his astonishing grasp of the German mentality and the German character. To that he added a penetrating understanding of his own people, and the will to criticize where necessary that which he loved beyond everything else. Thus he always thought of the German as an artist without the love of beauty, a skilled technician without love of the machine, a man born to the idea of Nietzsche and imbued with the myth of the Master Race, yet one who had a pathetic need for friendship and even love, a man who should be completely an individualist, yet one who gave his blind obedience to any overlord who cared to seize power and wield it.

Against this de Gaulle set the Frenchman—the brilliant producer of ideas who yet had not the urge or the need to carry them out, a man who planned his life logically and then proceeded to break all his own rules, a man who had a passionate love for his homeland, which was everything in life, yet who set out for the ends of the earth to found colonies which he attempted to make into France itself— a "hardworking lazybones," he called him.

From this full analysis of the character and will of his own people de Gaulle drew his inspiration for France's future. He saw in it the necessity for a constant state of military preparedness and military sufficiency; otherwise, he realized, it would mean the end of France. While other countries could rely on their immense material or technological resources, or on a great and growing population which could quickly wash over and erase the attenuating effects and the memory of defeats, France, just because her people were so volatile while they were still so unchanging, because they were temperamental while yet so coldly logical, had to fight always for her existence or disappear as a separate nation.

He drew his inspiration from the history of France that he knew so well. He turned to Cardinal Mazarin, the seventeenth-century diplomat who succeeded Richelieu and, when civil war tore open France, formed a great army under Marshal Turenne and ruled all France for more than eight years, during which he made an alliance with Cromwell, brought all the Rhine provinces under the control of France, gathered in a great part of French Flanders, and curbed the power of Spain.

De Gaulle found in the life of Léon-Michel Gambetta an inspiration for the future—and how much an inspiration it turned out to be! De Gaulle pointed to the fact that

when France had been humiliated at Sedan in 1870 and
the Prussian Army was drawn in a great circle around
Paris, Gambetta, then Minister of the Interior, escaped
from the capital in a balloon and, reaching Tours, set up
headquarters there, from which he carried on a resistance
on the part of the unsubjugated French.

Finally, and inevitably, for Clemenceau was an idol of
his youth, de Gaulle drew inspiration and guidance from
the old Jacobin's example in the First World War. Then
Georges Clemenceau, editor of the Parisian daily newspaper *L'Aurore,* so bitterly attacked the Government for
its shortcomings in not producing adequate supplies for
the Army, and for not taking a firm enough hand over the
defeatism which swept France increasingly as the situation grew worse, that he was finally called on by President
Poincaré to take power as Prime Minister and throw every
possible effort into the battle.

De Gaulle was certain that if Germany attacked it
would be true to form—the lightning thrust, the powerful
first blow aimed at crushing all opposition, and then the
swift breakthrough. His study of history showed him that
this had been the German pattern from Frederick the
Great, Moltke, and Schlieffen. "To-day Germany plans to
use all the means at her disposal for a rapid breakthrough," he said.

De Gaulle had become friendly with Gaston Palewski,
the chief assistant to Paul Reynaud, then Minister of
Justice. Palewski arranged a meeting between the two
men in which Reynaud, who had read *L'Armée de métier*
and completely agreed with de Gaulle's views, could question the author at great length. That was to be the first of
many meetings, and it was a turning-point in de Gaulle's
life.

9

France Rejects the Plan

❖ When de Gaulle, in 1934, agreed to meet Reynaud he realized that he was taking a great chance with his military career. It was an unusual situation in which he found himself—an officer on active duty whose job was closely connected with the Ministry of Defense attempting to persuade a Member of Parliament that the French defensive plans were all wrong and that his own should be adopted.

But there was nothing strange about it in the mind of de Gaulle, who was so firmly convinced of the rightness of his theories that he was prepared to risk anything to give France the opportunity of getting to know them. In this he was, as usual, supported by his wife, who, though she always tried to hold herself aloof from politics, and from military matters, was so sure that her husband was right that she felt it essential that he should do everything he could to convince his critics and the millions of skeptics that France, unless she listened to the new prophet, was in mortal danger.

Those first meetings between de Gaulle and Reynaud were exploratory. The short, squat politician and the tall soldier met at Reynaud's office, No. 5 Place du Palais-Bourbon, behind the Chamber of Deputies, where Reynaud was making his name as an eloquent and forceful speaker, or at the politician's home, No. 47 rue du Faubourg-Saint-Honoré. "I agree generally with what you say, Colonel—in fact, my own theories are very similar—but I must absorb all your ideas if I am to put them before the Assembly," Reynaud told de Gaulle. So meeting followed meeting, with the effervescent politician listening intently, thumbs hooked into his waistcoat and fingers splayed like fans. The lean, sad-faced army officer, only his eyes showing the intensity of his feelings, explained in minute detail every facet of the problem.

Palewski was an invaluable help to both men at that time. As the weeks passed he could see that the theories of de Gaulle were becoming more and more those of Reynaud, until in time they were not only inseparable, but Reynaud was prepared to carry his campaign for their acceptance to the extreme, to advise their adoption in a speech in the Assembly. The three men conferred for a long time before it was agreed that no other course would break down the opposition of politicians and soldiers alike.

"I feel that we should take this gamble because Hitler is increasing his power in Germany at such a pace that France will be defenseless within a few years," said de Gaulle. "But how to convince General Maurin [the War Minister] and Marshal Pétain?"

Pétain, although he was still a great admirer of de Gaulle personally, was becoming increasingly at variance with his views. The old soldier—as conservative as most of his school—felt that there was no logic in the new theories, and, in fact, went out of his way to warn French leaders against the dangers of listening to what were almost heresies in his eyes. The old Marshal had thought of taking de Gaulle with him, as his assistant, in 1934, when Pétain was called into the Doumergue Cabinet, but there were too many voices raised in opposition.

By this time Charles and Yvonne de Gaulle had found a house of their own where they could build the family life which was made more essential by the continued ill-health of their daughter Anne. They found their home in the village of Colombey-les-Deux Eglises, on the fringe of the Champagne country of Lorraine, about a hundred and fifty miles from Paris. La Boisserie, the house that they found for sale, was a comparatively small dwelling in a pleasant little park, but it had the advantage from the point of view of the de Gaulles that it was shielded from the road by trees and yet at the back had an uninterrupted view of farmland.

There are twelve rooms in La Boisserie, and also a small turret—not much of a fortress, but a room sufficiently large to form de Gaulle's study and give him the chance, in his thoughtful moments, to look out over the rolling countryside of his France. Soon the quiet couple in the big house were known to all of Colombey's 365 people, and they have been friends, but not close friends, ever since. Mme. de Gaulle entered into the life of the village to a limited but friendly extent, and the villagers, recognizing her love of seclusion, were content to leave it at that. With her was Mlle. Marguerite Potel, nurse to Anne since the child, born while the de Gaulles were with the Army of the Rhine at Trier, was two years old.

Despite the fact that they had found the home they had been looking for for many years, the de Gaulles were often absent from it in Paris. De Gaulle's post at the Ministry of Defense and the urge that was in him to make France take notice of his new theories made it imperative that he should be more often in the capital than at home. Yvonne de Gaulle accepted this situation with the same good sense that she had shown in the face of every other major event of her life. She has said, "My mission in life is to make a happy home for my husband," and she has never failed in that task. Always at hand when he needed companionship, but never in the limelight, she has yet exercised a considerable influence on her famous husband for the very reason that he has learned to respect her common sense and her insight which no love for him has ever been allowed to cloud. De Gaulle willingly and gratefully admits the debt he owes to his wife for her advice and foresight as much as for her unfailing loyalty and love.

He needed all the domestic support he could have during the disappointing months of 1935. Then France's leaders were all too ready to believe that Adolf Hitler was bluffing them, and that German strength was only a myth. In the face of the undoubted strength of the Maginot Line, the soldier of France believed that an attack by Germany was unthinkable and foredoomed to failure. Reynaud backed de Gaulle to the limit. "His spirit is amazing," he said of him. "No matter what rebuffs he suffers, he is unruffled and continues as if nothing has happened. Sometimes I think he has too much spirit and too much will power."

It was on March 15, 1935, that Paul Reynaud finally took the tribune of the Assembly to press the merits of the de Gaulle theories. The Government, through the Prime Minister, Pierre Flandin, had invoked Article 40 of the law of 1928, which gave them the right to retain men in the colors for two years instead of the usual twelve months.

Reynaud intervened in the debate. The signs that Hitler intended to break his treaty obligations had convinced him that his fears regarding the inefficiency of the French military policy which he had expressed as long ago as

1924 were amply justified. He now traced the theories of
de Gaulle that the modern army must be composed of
highly trained professional soldiers, for the instruments
they would need to use were too delicate and too costly
to be handled by conscripts. "To-day it is necessary to
recast our military organization in order to deal with new
perils and new needs," he said. "It would be a miracle if
a system conceived for the conditions of Europe in 1927
would give us security in the Europe of 1935. In 1927 the
Germany of Stresemann was a member of the League of
Nations. The Germany of 1935 of Mr. Hitler is out of the
League, and her youth believes that there is no longer any
hope in peace, but still a little in war. I insist that we en-
list sufficient men to form ten divisions of specialist troops
—armored divisions of 500 tanks with supporting artillery
and anti-aircraft and self-contained air support.

"If war should break out to-morrow and Belgium is in-
vaded," Reynaud continued, "it would not be without
precedent. If we have not the means to take our troops
immediately to the eastern frontier to aid Belgium, and
also to help her to cover her eastern frontier, what will
happen to us? I believe things will take the same course
as they have in the past. It is not impossible for the Belgian Army to be driven into the sea. That would leave
350 kilometers of unprotected French frontier across the
north of the country to be defended. Is there any man
here who will admit that he is ready to see the richest
provinces of France overrun once more by the invader and
separated from the mother country? That is why the German press reacted only mildly when we spoke of increasing the length of military service, but reacted sharply at
the idea of our reorganizing our Army on modern lines."

In the public gallery de Gaulle sat with Palewski. His

face was inscrutable as the debate developed and it became apparent that, though there was support for Reynaud's suggestion, nothing would ever come of it. When
Reynaud continued to show that France was in danger
from the new Germany there was still no sign that the
Assembly was prepared to take either notice or positive
action.

Léon Blum immediately expressed the Socialist opposition to an armaments race and the rule of force. "We
continue to think that the real protection lies in mass
mobilization."

Maurin took the floor, and though his speech was destructive where Reynaud's had been constructive, it was
obvious that the Minister for War would carry the day.
"France bases her military preparations on defense rather
than offense," he cried. "To adopt M. Reynaud's suggestion would mean that we are preparing to take offensive
action. How much can one believe that we still dream of
taking the offensive when we have spent millions on es-
tablishing a fortified barrier across the north of France?
Would we not be mad to go forward of that barrier in
pursuit of I know not what adventure?" he asked.

This was a viewpoint that must succeed. Palewski
turned to de Gaulle. "We have lost," he groaned.

"On the contrary, we have had a very good day," replied de Gaulle. "The majority of the Deputies felt that
Reynaud was right, but were afraid to admit it in the face
of the condemnation of the General Staff and the Ministry
of Defense. But they will not forget what we have put
before them to-day, and we shall see to it that they hear
more and more in the future. No, Gaston, it has been a
very good day for us all."

Reynaud filed a rebuttal in the Chamber, demanding six

armored divisions, and this proposal was allowed to remain on the file until the following year, without anything being done about it.

The Commission of the Army rejected the project out of hand. It was stated that it was "useless, not desirable, and contrary to both logic and history." The Government agreed with the Commission, and when the project came up for public discussion on March 26 it was thrown out. In addition to that, Fabry, who had taken over the post of Minister for War, successfully proposed to the War Council that a portion of the money allotted to tanks in the Budget should be transferred to the purchase of more artillery for defense.

On July 15, 1935, General Debeney, the Army Chief of Staff, expressed in *La Revue des Deux Mondes* the viewpoint of the General Staff on the new theories of war advocated by Reynaud and de Gaulle. The General could see no value in the new type of armored division suggested by de Gaulle, save in offense. "And who would visualize an offensive action by the French Army into the heart of the Rhineland?" he asked.

> On such a field of operations what value would be such a specialized corps? We know the terrain, very mountainous and broken, wooded and densely populated. Did one visualize using the mobility of the new Army for a raid towards the Rhine? In a country which has nothing in common with the plains of Hungary or of Poland, where the roads pass constantly through inhabited places, in which the countryside beyond the towns and villages is covered with enclosed fields and trees, the speed of advance of a specialized corps would not be very great. Improvised obstacles would reduce very quickly the possibilities of maneuver, and these inconveniences are the least that one might expect. We would have a brilliant communiqué announcing the departure of the corps, and after a few days an SOS for help. Let us content ourselves with saluting the Army of the future only in the glorious halls of Les Invalides.

It was in 1936 that de Gaulle first met Léon Blum, then a Socialist M.P. In January 1935, writing in *Le Populaire,* Blum condemned the de Gaulle theories, and declared that, so far as he could see, their only use would be as an instrument of a *coup d'état.* In Blum's eyes at that time militarism was to be condemned: it was the natural enemy of the people.

A year later, when the two men met for the first time at the instance of Colonel Mayer, who took de Gaulle to see the Prime Minister at the Hôtel Matignon, de Gaulle explained in detail all those points on which Blum had reservations. The Prime Minister listened attentively to what the Colonel had to say. Finally, de Gaulle told him that it was necessary that France should be in a position to take the offensive should any danger threaten, and to do so it would be essential to adopt the only means by which any nation could take a rapid and effective offensive action—the new-style armored division. Blum looked into the grave eyes of the officer in front of him. "An army on the defensive is always an army in inferiority," de Gaulle told him.

Blum raised both hands towards the ceiling in the gesture of resignation. "You win, Colonel de Gaulle, but how would you suggest that I, a Socialist, and with France in the state in which we see her at present, propose that we should embrace a policy consistent with being the first to attack?"

And so, though de Gaulle had, in fact, won his battle to convince some of the political leaders of France that he was right, there was still no effort made or move planned to carry out his ideas.

Blum admitted years later in his memoirs that he had not had the foresight to recognize the strategic genius of de Gaulle. Instead he preferred to listen to the advice of his Chiefs of Staff, who, to a man, condemned the new theories as being revolutionary and dangerous. Pétain claimed that the development of tanks and aircraft had not in any way altered the basic principles of warfare. The security of France had always reposed on the maintenance of a defensive and continuous front, supported by a system of fortifications. That approach was unanimously supported among all the high officers of the General Staff. They were all convinced that tanks or armored cars should not be used except with the direct support of the artillery, by which means the whole defensive system of the enemy could be disorganized.

Blum, honest and troubled that all was not well, recorded his opinion that an army such as had been conceived by de Gaulle, with fast-moving divisions, would be irresistible and invulnerable, and could cut a way through the frontiers of the enemy as a squadron of cruisers cuts through the seas. He felt after all that these armored divisions constituted the ideal instrument for a system of collective security. He wondered what other system France could adopt to carry out its obligations in a case where she had no common frontier with the nation attacked. The difficulty would be even greater where France was separated from her allies by the aggressor nation.

But the defeat of the Reynaud suggestion in the Assembly meant also the temporary defeat of Colonel de Gaulle. He was punished. Maurin called to him at the end of a sitting of the National Defense Council, "Good-bye, de Gaulle. There is no place for you here."

To those who asked where de Gaulle would be sent the General said with heavy humor, "I shall send him to Corsica."

De Gaulle's seniority in the Army List was cut so that he did not attain the rank of full colonel until December 1937, when he was sent to Metz to take over the command of the 507th Armored Regiment. The official explanation for the removal of his name from the list of regular promotions was that he had been taken prisoner in the First World War, and therefore had not done as much for France as his contemporaries. This was a lame excuse which his fine war record made nonsense of.

But in Germany the lessons of the de Gaulle theory had not been allowed to pass unnoticed. General Guderian was charged by Hitler with producing a tank division which would have all the mobility of the one de Gaulle had envisaged. By the end of 1935 the first Panzer Division had taken shape. It contained a brigade of 540 tanks, as compared with the 500 planned by de Gaulle; a reconnaissance regiment, almost exactly as de Gaulle had suggested; five battalions of infantry, compared with the six of de Gaulle; a detachment of engineers, as outlined by de Gaulle; and a camouflage unit, also as planned by de Gaulle.

When Germany occupied the Rhineland in March 1936 France was still not convinced that de Gaulle was right; indeed he was in process of being punished for his temerity.

To say that de Gaulle had not been hurt by the turn of events would be to distort the facts. He was deeply wounded by the treatment he had received, even while he recognized that his unorthodox approach to the matter must always have brought punishment once he had failed. But he went to Metz feeling that the slight of the loss of seniority was a stain on his honor. This he could not tolerate.

In those first months while he was at Metz he withdrew

into himself to a degree abnormal even for him. Yvonne de Gaulle kept by him at every opportunity to ease his bitterness.

There was, luckily, a safety valve for de Gaulle in the need to bring his regiment to a high state of efficiency. As his unit advanced its technique, so he became more and more convinced that his own theories were right. He wrote in 1937:

> After several actual experiences I am more convinced than ever that the ideas I have tried to expound are well founded. But, alas, they are better received in Germany than in my own country. The age of the infantryman has passed, save in a defensive role. The artillery shield still has a relative value, but it is in support of tanks that it will be employed in the future above everything else. We are entering on the era of the mechanized army. All the prejudiced critics in the world will not stop it coming. Happily for us, the Germans also have their good military conformists who hamper the development of the Panzer Corps, aviation, and the Navy.

The technical skill and the high degree of training of the 507th Regiment attracted attention in Metz. General Giraud, G.O.C. of the garrison town, where 30,000 of France's best troops were stationed, came on a tour of inspection, and was staggered by what he saw. Here de Gaulle was demonstrating the truth of his theories. In the maneuvers of the 507th Regiment Giraud saw a new concept of war—rapid movement, concentrated firepower, swift development of forces, and ability to recover just as swiftly from a reverse.

Blum sent for de Gaulle once more. For hours the two men discussed mechanization and the new army. Blum was convinced at last, but it was too late to make up the lost time.

De Gaulle himself had been using his spare time at

Metz to finish his book *France and Her Army*, which convinced many thousands more. But again it was too late. France, which could have been two years ahead of any nation in the world in the new art of armored warfare, was now four years behind Germany in her own brand of organization.

The War Council decided on December 3, 1938, to equip two armored divisions on the de Gaulle pattern. But by then the German Panzers mustered twelve divisions. Hitler had also made all his plans, and his accomplice, Mussolini, had made his. France's one chance to stave off war in Europe had existed when de Gaulle first revolted against the "méthode a priori." If there had been men of foresight . . . It was when he thought of this that de Gaulle found himself beginning to turn against Pétain. Had he taken up the struggle for action as Reynaud had tried to do, there would have been no flamboyant entry into the Rhineland, no rape of Czechoslovakia, no conquests in Africa. France would have been indisputably the strongest Power on the mainland of Europe. As 1938 drew to a close she was one of the weakest. But still the General Staff saw no danger. Pétain was convinced that there could be no question of an invasion. Writing in the *Revue des Deux Mondes*, he declared: "The fortified front provided by the Maginot Line has given Europe a new stability. As for tanks, which are supposed to guarantee a short war—their failure is startling."

On the brink of war on July 4, 1939, Weygand, at a horse show at Lille, declared: "I believe that the Army of France to-day has a valor greater than at any moment in history. It possesses matériel of the first quality, fortifications of the first order, excellent morale, and a remarkable High Command. None of us desires war, but I affirm that if anyone insists on us gaining a new victory we shall gain one."

That also was Pétain's view. He wrote a preface to a book by General Chauvineau in which he said: "Our Army is in a position to strike a hard blow against any enemy who might wish to penetrate beyond our frontiers."

10

De Gaulle's Armor Halts the Germans

❧ When the German Panzers poured over the frontier into Poland on September 1, 1939, Colonel Charles de Gaulle was the officer commanding the tanks of the French Fifth Army at Wangenburg, in Alsace. He had the infuriating experience then of knowing that armored divisions of his own design were tearing the heart out of Polish resistance within a few days, and with very few casualties, just as he had so often predicted would happen. In those few days of September there could have been no doubt in the mind of anyone with any knowledge of military matters who was the father of the mechanized division. The pattern was all as de Gaulle had forecast, the numbers of men and weapons employed so much of his choosing that there could be no argument.

De Gaulle decided that even if it was now too late to give France the advantage it might still be possible to save her from complete disaster. He was at no time misled by the inactivity on the Western Front. In letters to his friends of the Dumesnil circle he repeatedly pointed out the dangers about to break over France. On the suggestion of Reynaud he set about preparing a Secret Memorandum for submission to the Prime Minister, Edouard Daladier, and other leading public figures. Nothing daunted de Gaulle, and he did not worry that his action would be construed as a breach of discipline on the part

of a serving soldier. As usual, he gave the greatest thought
to the construction of the sentences, spending time over
the punctuation. "Bad punctuation can ruin a good sentence," he often says.

After pointing out that the German Army found it easy
to overrun Poland, a nation of thirty-five million people
with a great military tradition, he said:

> To break an attack by a mechanized force only a mechanized
> force has any certain efficiency. The massive counterattack of aerial
> and land squadrons directed against an adversary with freedom
> of movement demands the use of modern defensive methods. . . .
> If the enemy has not already built up a mechanized force suf-
> ficient to break through our lines he soon will. The startling suc-
> cess of his motorized divisions in Poland will encourage him to
> try again in the new way. Now it is necessary that we should
> realize that the Maginot Line, for all the reinforcements that it
> has received and will receive, whatever the quantities of infantry
> and artillery which occupy it or support it, is capable of being
> overcome. Tanks employed *en masse* are capable of overrunning
> our defenses, active and passive. . . .
> It is essential to create new armored and mechanized divisions.
> On land, fast divisions and divisions of the line, each provided
> with tanks in sufficient number and powerful enough, armored
> infantry, enough artillery to sustain themselves in battle, equipped
> with all the means of breakthrough and movement necessary to
> overcome the obstacles which the enemy and the terrain would
> place against them, and provided with special vehicles which
> would clear the roads for the transports and supplies. In the air,
> assault divisions capable in the course of the battle of maintaining
> a position and of swooping down on the enemy to attack on land
> or water, and of long-range squadrons capable of attacking the
> industrial vitals of the enemy. The combination of these land and
> air forces will permit large ruptures of the enemy lines, wide-
> spread maneuvers, and the ability to exploit the gains. By these
> means a new strategy will be born, on the land, on the sea, and
> in the air. . . .

This Secret Memorandum, or Explanatory Note, was
submitted to Daladier. In fact, he had already received

news of it when a letter from de Gaulle to Reynaud through Palewski had been opened by the Army censor and passed to the Prime Minister's office. In it de Gaulle also dealt briefly with his idea that there should be a co-ordinated committee of every one connected with defense, so that the war effort could be speeded up and given some kind of cohesion. Daladier, not unnaturally, was furious, but as much with Reynaud, whom he accused of con-spiring against him, as with de Gaulle. In the end it was Palewski who was made the scapegoat, and was forced to resign his position as secretary to Reynaud, whose cordial relations with Daladier were thereupon restored.

The eighty politicians and generals to whom de Gaulle sent his Memorandum ignored his warning.

It was not until March 21, 1940, that the Daladier Government was overthrown, and two days later Reynaud formed a Government. He immediately sent for de Gaulle and from him obtained an appreciation of the situation which he could place before the National Assembly. But there was little sign that even now the Deputies realized the dangers of the military situation. Only Blum really spoke with eloquence in support of Reynaud's views. However, the new Prime Minister obtained a majority in the voting which followed.

De Gaulle was kept in Paris for a few days to advise Reynaud, and was given an office in the Quai d'Orsay. What he saw at that time in Government circles filled him with even greater dismay, for he could trace clearly the disintegration of French public life: the people were being led inexorably by their political leaders, the press, and their trade unions to the idea of capitulation in the fight against Hitler Germany. Behind all this there loomed the figure and influence of his old friend and leader,

Marshal Pétain, now Ambassador to Spain. In this post the old soldier was in a perfect position to act as the messenger for Franco, the go-between for Hitler in his negotiations with the Government of France.

At that stage the last shreds of loyalty which de Gaulle still had for Pétain disappeared. From that time Pétain was in de Gaulle's eyes an enemy of France, and one to be fought at all costs. De Gaulle believed that age had sapped the courage of the old soldier, but considered it unforgivable. De Gaulle knew now that the fall of Reynaud would mean the end of French resistance, and that Pétain was planning to take over power, perhaps with the help of his friend Pierre Laval.

Reynaud and de Gaulle had many long and anxious talks in those days. The politician, whose admiration for the gifts of leadership and of common sense of the soldier was boundless, himself relied to an increasing extent on de Gaulle's advice. But the Prime Minister was held in office by the usual coalition of parties, and was therefore unable to act exclusively on his own initiative. Daladier, who opposed almost every one of Reynaud's ideas, was his Minister of Defense.

"I want to form a Coordinated Committee for War, such as you have suggested," Reynaud told de Gaulle, "and I want you to be its secretary. You will be responsible not only for arranging meetings of all the Ministers connected with defense, but also of the Service commanders. You will draw up the agenda, and will see that all decisions arrived at are carried through quickly. In that way at last we shall be able to get something done."

De Gaulle knew that such a suggestion would never be acceptable to Daladier. And, sure enough, when it was put to the Minister of Defense, he replied, "If de Gaulle comes here I shall resign, and I shall tell Reynaud that he can appoint his nominee in my place."

De Gaulle, though disappointed, was not surprised by this outburst. After one more long talk with Reynaud he prepared to return to his unit in Alsace. But instead he was ordered to report to General Gamelin at his headquarters at the Château de Vincennes. There the Commander-in-Chief lived and worked, in de Gaulle's own words, "as if he were in a monastery," cut off from all active participation in the life of the army. General Georges commanded the army of the Northeast from La Ferté-sous-Jouarre, and under him was part of the General Staff. The rest of the General Staff were with General Doumenc at Montry. To de Gaulle the idea that an army could be directed from three separate headquarters was not only unthinkable, but highly dangerous. "There can be no guarantee either of coordinated command or of coordinated action in such circumstances," he said to Reynaud.

"I am raising the number of our armored divisions from two to four," Gamelin told de Gaulle. "And I have decided that you shall command the Fourth as from May 15."

De Gaulle knew a fierce pride when he heard this. To be promoted from colonel to major-general was an honor he had never expected after his intransigence to authority. But he could not resist telling Gamelin, even as he thanked him for his faith in him, that he feared that it might be too late to try to transform France's armored strength. Gamelin told him that he felt that his fears were completely unjustified.

As de Gaulle continued on his way towards his unit in Alsace the thought that the Commander-in-Chief was still confident that the old-fashioned French Army could stand any chance against the new mechanized Army of Germany saddened and alarmed him. And when the German blitzkrieg began on May 10, and the German armored divisions with their lorried infantry swept across the Ardennes and gained the banks of the Meuse within three days, de Gaulle knew that he was right, and that the battle was already virtually lost.

On May 11 he was ordered to take over the Fourth Division, a nonexistent unit, and, as foreshadowed by Gamelin, was told to report at General Doumenc's headquarters. "You are charged with delaying the enemy advance in the region of Laon to enable General Touchon to establish a front on the Aisne and the Ailette which will bar the way to Paris. You will be under direct command of General Georges, who will see that you have the necessary forces to carry out your task."

As de Gaulle—at forty-nine the youngest general in the French Army—drove away for his meeting with Georges he realized that already the idea of defeat was in the minds of some members of the General Staff. Doumenc, who had learned that two of France's armored divisions had been annihilated, was justifiably despondent.

Georges looked crushed when de Gaulle got to him. "You forecast all this a long time ago, de Gaulle," Georges said to the newest French general. "Now it is time for you to act."

Major-General de Gaulle had very little with which to act, but he proceeded at once to Laon, and there in the little village of Bruyères, southeast of the town, he set up his headquarters without a headquarters staff. He was dressed in the leather jacket of the tank officer, and carried no insignia of his rank, but he suggested authority in everything he did and said. Soon the few men who composed his division knew that they had a leader among them. He seemed calm—ice-cold, in fact—and only his incessant smoking of cigarettes betrayed any feeling in him. Inwardly he was boiling with rage. As he went forward to make his first contacts with the enemy, and to take up once more his First World War role of reconnaissance, he was met by a steady stream of refugees pouring westward and southward away from the frightening dive-bombing aircraft and from the rumbling tanks. There were French soldiers among them, men who had no fight left in them. They had been ordered to throw away their rifles by the German Army. "We haven't time to stop to take you prisoner," the Germans had joked as they swept past the defeated men. This made de Gaulle angrier than anything else. The insult to France was almost more than he could tolerate, and he thought only of showing the enemy that they could not take liberties with the French Army in this way. But as he realized how small were his resources he wondered how it was to be done.

Gradually the components of his new division began to come into the area. While the members of his staff got them roughly into units, de Gaulle went forward to the banks of the Sissonne irrigation canal. He passed on the way a few elements of the Third Cavalry Division, the Fourth Group of Artillery, and a few riflemen who were deployed along the length of the canal to try to hold it against a crossing by the enemy.

As de Gaulle stood on the banks of the canal and looked eastward a rifle bullet whined past his head, and the flashes from the trees on the other side showed him that the enemy was already there, though he could not determine from that in what strength. But he was satisfied that the marshes to the east would prevent any use of tanks for a river crossing. Only the road bridge was suitable for such vehicles.

Soon he had three battalions of tanks—one of B2 heavy tanks and two of Renault light tanks. He decided that, small though his force was, it was imperative that he should attack at once to try to disorganize the enemy while he was preparing for the next phase of his advance. He had no infantry, no artillery which could move with him, and no anti-aircraft cover.

Few commanders would have contemplated a major operation of assault with such ill-assorted troops. Despite the handicap, de Gaulle was acting on his principles: he had preached the value of surprise, rapid movement, and thrust too often to feel that he should now be cautious. On the morning of May 18 he gave the order to attack towards the northeast, with the object of capturing Sissonne and Montcornet, which straddled the roads to Saint-Quentin, Laon, and Rheims, and which would bar the enemy way to the west and to the front held by the French Sixth Army.

His boldness took the enemy by surprise. The light tanks reached Montcornet, and the heavies successfully captured the village of Chivres and reached the outskirts of Saint-Pierremont. But that was the limit of the advance for the moment. The Germans were in too great strength, and their artillery in Montcornet inflicted the most serious casualties on the light tanks of the French. De Gaulle withdrew his forces a short way into the woods south of the river and near Agincourt.

The Fourth Battalion of Chasseurs had just reached de Gaulle, tired through over-much travelling and ill-equipped, but he felt compelled to ask them for one more effort in the neighborhood of Chivres. With this new sup-

port a column of thirty German lorries carrying infantry
was overrun and completely destroyed.

A huge concentration of artillery and wave after wave
of Stuka dive bombers were now called up by the Germans to bear on the Fourth Division as they desperately
sought to regain the initiative and force the French back
to their original lines. But de Gaulle, everywhere on the
front, inspiring his tired and sometimes badly shocked
men by his calmness and his confidence, refused to be
driven back. And now he realized that the opportunity
was there for an immediate attack by the French units on
his flanks. He sent hurried messages to them giving them
the situation as he saw it, and urging them to take advantage of his success. But these men, timid and dis-
pirited, refused to move from the defensive lines they had
taken up. De Gaulle, his men coming under more and
more pressure as the Germans threw in extra reserves,
found himself occupying a dangerous salient in the German front, and was forced to come back behind the line
of the Sissonne canal. All he could claim for his brilliant
action was that he had delayed the German advance for
a whole day, and had inflicted heavy casualties on the
enemy while taking 130 prisoners. His own losses were
fewer than 200 men. But if the French commanders on
his flanks had had a small proportion of his boldness a
major victory might have been won.

De Gaulle knew from intelligence reports that the situation was desperate: that the Dutch Army had disappeared, that the Belgian Army was falling back fast to the
west, and that the British and the First French Army,
operating in Belgium, were cut off from France. On May
19 General Gamelin was replaced by General Weygand,
who immediately set off for Belgium with the idea of re-

uniting the two Allied fronts. De Gaulle and his battered Fourth Division were ordered to pull back towards the west, and during the night of May 26-27 he received the order to proceed immediately to Abbeville and there to attack the enemy, who had established a bridgehead to the south of the city.

The Fourth Division had been continually on the move for ten days, and it was in a sorry state of tiredness and lack of equipment. There was a battalion of heavy tanks, one of light tanks, the Seventh Regiment of Dragons portés, a group of 105 howitzers, a battery of anti-aircraft guns, and five anti-tank batteries. Only the light-tank units were up to strength, and all the others were made up of hastily collected troops, many of them untrained for the work they had on hand.

Yet the spirit of the division was tremendous, and it stemmed almost entirely from the example of General de Gaulle. He it was who was seen by all his men continually throughout the long hours of the march. He seemed to be tireless, and able to be everywhere at the same time. His officers were inspired to emulate his example, and his men responded, as men always will to great leadership.

De Gaulle decided to attack at once. Deprived of the element of surprise so far as his position was concerned, he seized the one opportunity remaining to him, that of surprising the enemy by attacking without attempting to regroup or to deploy. He sent his troops in against Huppy in the west, the woods of Limeux and Bailleul in the center, and Bray-les-Mareuil in the east. By nightfall the Fourth Division had captured Huppy and Limeux, but de Gaulle was not satisfied and pushed on, dividing his forces and attacking, on the left, Moyenneville and Bienfay; in the center, Huchenneville and Villers; and, on the right, Mareuil, with an oblique thrust by the heavy tanks from west to east to take them behind the rear of the German forces in order to prise them loose from Mont Caubert.

The fighting was heavy and bloody. Outnumbered and outgunned, the Fourth Division fought with brilliance and bravery, and de Gaulle was always in the forefront of the engagement, directing personally what had become almost hand-to-hand fighting.

By nightfall again every objective had been attained, but at the heaviest cost. Shattered tanks and vehicles were everywhere, and there were French and enemy dead thick in the fields. Yet the Fourth Division celebrated its victory that night as the German forces withdrew from contact. Major Gehring, a German who described the battle, later declared, "Our anti-tank units fought heroically, but the effects of their efforts were considerably reduced by the valor of the French tank crews. Our anti-tank defenses were overwhelmed, and our infantry had to concede the battle. A terror of the tanks seized our soldiers, and our losses were heavy."

A special Order of the Day was issued by General Weygand citing de Gaulle for his handling of the battles of Laon and Abbeville: "This gallant and energetic officer attacked with his division the bridgehead of Abbeville, solidly held by the enemy. He broke the German resistance and advanced fourteen kilometers through the enemy lines, taking hundreds of prisoners and capturing considerable matériel."

The Fourth Division gathered itself again, but on the following day was faced by completely new German troops, who were again reinforced on the following day. But still de Gaulle went into the attack. His men were met by a murderous fire from artillery, and Stukas continually screamed down on them from the sky. Still the French fought their way up the slopes of Mont Caubert. Yet the crest defied them, and the Germans, rushing up reinforcements, counterattacked viciously. The Fourth Division, however, held on to all its gains until relieved on May 30 by the British 51st Highland Division. De Gaulle now pulled his battered Fourth Division back to Beauvais to regroup.

He and his men could claim possibly the only advance in the whole Battle of France—the only victory over the enemy, and the only occasion on which French territory was regained and held against the all-conquering Panzers.

But the battle was lost. Of that de Gaulle had now no doubt. The King of the Belgians had capitulated with all his forces, the evacuation of Dunkirk was under way, and the French Army had practically disintegrated.

It was in that situation that de Gaulle came to his decision to carry on the fight outside territorial France—in the Empire, anywhere where it was possible to rally Frenchmen to the banner. At that moment he remembered the lines of his ancestor Charles de Gaulle: "In a camp surprised by night by an attack, where every man struggles in isolation, one does not ask what is the rank of him who raises the flag and shouts the first rallying call."

Before he had taken the Fourth Division into battle on May 18 de Gaulle had sent an urgent message to his family. He instructed his wife to pack up immediately and go with the children to Carantec, in Brittany, and there to stay with an aunt. The message arrived on May 19, and Yvonne de Gaulle did not question the decision. She knew that "immediately" to her husband meant just that, and she left the same afternoon.

On June 1 de Gaulle was summoned to Weygand at Montry. There the Commander-in-Chief told de Gaulle plainly and simply that the next German offensive would come on June 6 on the Somme and the Aisne. "If we can recover quickly the men who escaped from Dunkirk, if the British can return to take part in the struggle, and the Royal Air Force can play its proper part in the battle, we still have a chance," he said.

De Gaulle knew that Weygand was deluding himself with his hopes. He thought to himself that Weygand, never an active commander of large bodies of men, had not the outlook to comprehend the situation. Weygand was a second-in-command in a Commander-in-Chief's chair, and the position was beyond him. All this made the young General's thoughts even more somber as he made his way back to his division.

11

Flight to England

❧ De Gaulle spent a week at Beauvais, during which time the news grew more bitter and harder to bear. France had lost fifteen divisions of her best troops, and the enemy was now preparing himself for the final blow. At midnight on June 6 a message arrived at the headquarters of the Fourth Division ordering de Gaulle immediately to Paris to see Reynaud.

The Prime Minister at last was no longer prepared to temporize over the appointment of de Gaulle to a key position in national defense. He offered the General the post of Under-Secretary of State to the Minister of National Defense, and de Gaulle accepted at once on condition that there was no question that the Cabinet would even consider the matter of surrender to the Germans. "If the battle of 1940 is lost," de Gaulle said to Reynaud, "then we must win some other battle." He then outlined his proposals for an evacuation of the necessary forces to North Africa, where the struggle could be continued.

Reynaud agreed with de Gaulle entirely. "I shall send you immediately to London to confer with Winston Churchill," he promised. "Meanwhile set to work on your mission. I shall want from Churchill an assurance of continued land and air support, and you in return can give him my assurance that your very presence is a guarantee that we shall continue the fight."

De Gaulle set to work without delay in his office in the rue Saint-Dominique. But soon he became conscious once again of the atmosphere of defeatism among French leaders, and that Pétain and Paul Baudouin were actively intriguing against Reynaud.

De Gaulle found it very difficult to work in the same Government as Pétain, who had returned to Paris in May, and whom he now distrusted. He knew that Pétain was determined to give way to the German threats, and that in his position of Vice-Premier he had great power. But, in fact, there was no reason for the two men to meet. De Gaulle realized, too, that the Countess Hélène de Portes, a middle-aged friend of Reynaud's, was an influence on the side of capitulation, and de Gaulle did not underestimate her influence with Reynaud.

In those few days before he flew to London to see Churchill, de Gaulle reached the heights of character and will. Everywhere in high circles he was assailed by doubting men and betrayed by intrigues. With the exception of a few Ministers, including Louis Marin and Georges Mandel, de Gaulle was alone in attempting to keep alive Reynaud's determination.

He learned with disgust of the efforts of Pétain to co-operate with the Germans. The Marshal had transmitted to President Roosevelt, by way of the American Ambassador in Paris, William Bullitt, the opinion that Britain was, in fact, planning to make a separate peace with Germany after "fighting to the last drop of French blood." This was an accusation which was cleverly spread by an active Fifth Column throughout France, and it was a taunt which British troops had often to endure throughout the fateful days of June, when France went down to defeat.

De Gaulle taxed Reynaud with this matter, declaring that it was close to treason. He persuaded the Prime Minister to appeal directly to Roosevelt for support.

On June 9 de Gaulle was flown to London for his first meeting with the British Prime Minister. With him was his aide-de-camp, Lieutenant (later General) Geoffroy de Courcel. It was a Sunday when they arrived, but de Gaulle was driven straight to 10 Downing Street. There two men who are so similar in thought and will, but so different in physical characteristics, came face to face. Each was immediately impressed, and each man gained a feeling of affection for the other which no changes of fortune, no difficulties of international politics, have destroyed.

Churchill was astonished at the calmness of his visitor in view of his known passionate attachment to the cause of France. De Gaulle talked and listened as if he were engaged in a peacetime sitting of his work group at the Staff College. Churchill, more ebullient, but none the less also down to earth and practical, matched him in his earnestness.

The British Prime Minister expressed his doubts that France could continue the struggle in view of the enormity of her defeat and the attitude of her political leaders. Nor would Churchill agree to sending a part of the Royal Air Force to metropolitan France. No persuasion on the part of de Gaulle would alter his mind on these points.

De Gaulle returned to Paris without any real achievements beyond words of encouragement and promises of the utmost possible assistance. On June 11 the French Government left Paris for Tours in the face of the advancing German Panzers, and at the same time Reynaud received word that Churchill was flying to Briare, on the Loire, to meet Weygand, and to see, at the front itself, what was the military situation.

It was now that de Gaulle insisted that Weygand must be replaced, and he refused to allow Reynaud to temporize further. "It would be madness to allow the British Prime Minister to discuss the military situation with a man who is already committed to capitulation," de Gaulle urged.

While Reynaud hurried to meet Churchill, de Gaulle took the Prime Minister's letter of appointment as Commander-in-Chief to General Huntziger, commander of the army group holding the center of the French line. Huntziger readily agreed to de Gaulle's offer of the position of Commander-in-Chief of a France fighting from African soil. But when de Gaulle again contacted Reynaud at Briare it was to find that once more the Prime Minister had hesitated over replacing Weygand.

De Gaulle hurried out after this meeting, convinced that at last he must begin to take matters into his own hands. Outside he met Pétain, who sarcastically congratulated him on his elevation to the rank of general at the moment of defeat. For once de Gaulle was stung to retort. "I would remind you, Marshal Pétain, that you yourself had the same experience in 1914, but not long afterwards came the battle of the Marne and finally victory," he said.

In the Cabinet conference which followed Pétain did his utmost to ensure that France and Britain would go their separate ways. Repeatedly he drew attention to the small amount of help France had received from Britain, and in this he was supported by Reynaud, who again demanded that the British Air Force should be sent to the help of the French forces. De Gaulle fought strenuously to keep Reynaud resolute and committed to continuing the struggle.

De Gaulle, in the face of the now almost absolute defeatism of a majority of the French Government, still worked on his vast plan for the evacuation of French forces to Africa and the continuation of the struggle from there. Meanwhile members of the Government themselves were concerned only with their next move and where they should set up their next headquarters. Most favored Bordeaux, but de Gaulle insisted that it must be Brittany, with Quimper his idea of the actual spot—the Breton Redoubt. As usual, he was able to convince Reynaud that his ideas were more logical than the others, but he was powerless when it came to keeping the Prime Minister to that course in the face of the continued barrage from the open advocates of capitulation. On June 12 de Gaulle knew that he had failed and that Bordeaux would be the new seat of government.

Roosevelt cabled Reynaud on June 13 that he was most impressed by the declaration that France would fight on on behalf of democracy even though it meant deliberate withdrawal, even to the Atlantic and North Africa. "I have been greatly heartened by what Mr. Churchill said a few days ago pledging continued resistance by the British Empire, and I am sure this determination applies equally to the great French Empire throughout the world," said the President.

Churchill came to Tours on the same day, and made the most impressive declaration of faith and friendship for France. "The cause of France will always remain dear to us, and we shall restore her in all her strength and dignity if we triumph," he insisted.

There was, however, much ineffectual talk on both sides at the conference which took place. Churchill cited the lessons of history to urge the importance of the French Army holding on as long as possible. "Every day gained counts," he insisted. Weygand agreed that every day gained counted, but declared that in his view it was now a matter of hours, not days. Pétain declared that there could be no comparison between the situation in 1918 and that of 1940. Anthony Eden, the Secretary for War, revealed that "an important neutral person" (Roosevelt) had informed Lord Halifax on June 7 that the losses of the Germans had been extremely heavy, and that there was no enthusiasm in Germany for the war. The British Government attached great significance to this report, said Eden.

It was the alleged lack of support of the British Air Force which led to the most controversial of the discussions. Churchill felt that it would be wrong to throw in the Royal Air Force, as suggested by General Georges, to drive the enemy back on the Marne and to hold him while reserves were organized. "It is essential to conserve intact the Royal Air Force, which I regard as the instrument on which depends, perhaps, the intervention of the United States in the conflict," he said.

"History will say without doubt that the Battle of France was lost through want of aircraft," Reynaud declared.

"Also through want of tanks and through the numerical superiority of the enemy," Churchill added.

Reynaud once more argued that the British air forces could render their best service if they were stationed in France, and to this Churchill replied that, while he would look into this question on his return to England, he would point out that many British planes had been lost on the ground in France through the German bombardment.

"We are always thankful, but we are also starved," Reynaud commented.

It was then that de Gaulle entered the discussion in an effort to bring it to a level which he felt could add something useful to the results. "Do you not think that the armor of your light tanks is insufficient, which renders them of little use in battle?" he asked Churchill. When the British Prime Minister promised to look into the matter on his return, de Gaulle went on, "And do you not think, sir, that certain elements of the British division which disembarked at Le Havre in May could usefully be amalgamated with certain of our own to form a most effective fighting force?" This also was considered a suggestion that might be taken up without delay, but the talk then turned to de Gaulle's Breton Redoubt.

"Do you not think it possible for us to establish a bridgehead on the Atlantic?" Churchill asked Reynaud.

"The matter is being studied," Weygand answered for the Prime Minister, "but it poses two difficulties—strategically and in the matter of supply. Brittany gives the Army little room for maneuver, and also 70 per cent of France's supply and victualling establishments are in the Paris area.

"It is true," Weygand said, "that Brittany is in communication with Britain, but it contains no arms factories and no resources. They could not hold out long there, because the enemy air forces, operating in a confined space, would make life untenable."

Churchill sensed that the feeling of the meeting—with the exception of de Gaulle, whose suggestions had been designed to allow the fight to be taken up again—was that the cause was lost. "If it is found impossible to continue the war from one of the many regions of France, would it not be possible to organize guerrilla warfare which would disperse the forces of the enemy in the same way as those of France have been dispersed, and would, in fact, perhaps be more damaging to him than any other form of resistance?" Churchill asked.

"If we can do this, find a method of hindering the tanks, and maintain a bridgehead on the Atlantic, we may gain the months necessary to obtain the intervention of the Americans," said Churchill.

"All that would lead to the destruction of France," declared Pétain, and Reynaud added that the towns would suffer greatly.

"It is easy to express oneself when one's country has not yet suffered and is unaware of the tortures which France has actually experienced," agreed Churchill, "but we wish to share the suffering of France and to experience the same tortures. We will not stop our efforts if the Army of France is forced to give in. With our Air Force and our Navy we shall, with our Empire, be able to inflict the most serious blockade on Europe and hold on for years. What will happen in this case to the French fleet? Britain has free use of the seas; her Empire and the French Empire are intact; the Belgian and Dutch possessions are dependent on her. We could develop rapidly a war of continents. It is possible that the Nazis will dominate Europe, but it will be a Europe in revolt, and it can be freed by the fall of a regime sustained above all by the victory of its machines."

There were general exchanges of platitudes following this typical rallying speech of Churchill's. De Gaulle found himself in complete agreement with everything the British Prime Minister had said—it might have been his own plan that Churchill had outlined—the guerrilla activity at home, the continuing battle from overseas, the Atlantic bridgehead, the employment of all the resources, economic and strategic, of the Empire.

The stench of defeat was growing stronger and the spirit of capitulation more powerful. In all this terrible situation, with France's western cities and towns filling up with thousands of hopeless and spiritless refugees, de

Gaulle grew immeasurably in stature. Arriving in Bordeaux on June 14, de Gaulle was anxious to know if Reynaud, having changed his mind, was still bent on going to North Africa to continue the fight. "I am certainly going to Algiers to set up government there," Reynaud replied.

"Then I shall go to London at once and arrange all the necessary ships for the transfer," de Gaulle told him. "Where will you be when I return?"

"I shall be in Algiers," Reynaud assured him.

Reynaud and de Gaulle had also discussed the question of the hundreds of German airmen who were at present in French hands. Churchill had asked at the conference at Tours that if and when France capitulated there should be no question that this would leave the prisoners on French soil, so that they could be put back into the air against the Royal Air Force. "I ask that you send them first to England," the British Prime Minister had said.

On this trip to London de Gaulle was instructed to ask what plans were being made for these prisoners and to what extent the British could transport them to English prison camps.

Before going to Brest to board the ship which would take him to Britain de Gaulle telephoned Admiral Darlan and spoke to him on the question of the ships needed to transport the French Army to North Africa. "The Prime Minister wants you to go to Bordeaux to-morrow to discuss the matter with him," de Gaulle told Darlan.

"What good can he do in Bordeaux?" exclaimed Darlan. "In any case, I'm busy—I have a Navy to command, and I have no time to waste talking over such harebrained schemes. How do you carry 800,000 men to North Africa— by levitation?"

De Gaulle asked whether Darlan wished him to inform

the Prime Minister that he did not intend to answer the
summons to Bordeaux, and the Admiral then replied, "Oh,
no; I'll go there, of course."

De Gaulle sailed from Brest in the destroyer "Milan" on
June 15, and reached London by way of Plymouth early on
June 16. He was immediately in conference with Eden,
and received the first news of an important offer Churchill
was to make to France—the permanent union between
Britain and France, in which everything, military and
economic, could be thrown into the common effort.

But by the time de Gaulle had flown back to Bordeaux
that same evening Reynaud had been overthrown, and
Pétain was Prime Minister, with Chautemps as Vice-
Premier, Darlan as Minister of the Navy, and Weygand as
Minister of Defense. De Gaulle realized then that nothing
more could be done. He had already sufficient proof that
Darlan had repeatedly taken action which hampered the
French war effort in the last days of the struggle.

As he walked the streets of the city de Gaulle had almost
the feeling that he was in enemy territory. He knew well
that he was now under surveillance and that plans were
afoot to arrest him, just as others who wanted to continue
the struggle were soon to be arrested. As he listened to the
anxious talk of people on the pavements his heart was
filled with bitterness. But he made no attempt to approach
any of his old friends. He had seen Pétain two nights before at dinner in the dining room of the Hôtel Splendide,
and, leaving the room after his own meal, had paused to
salute his old chief. Pétain had grasped him by the hand
and let it fall without a word of greeting or of farewell.

De Gaulle's mind was made up. Now he carefully
planned the few hours that remained for him in France.
He made no attempt to get in touch with his wife in the

house at Carantec. Their plans had long since been made. De Gaulle had arranged all their passports in the days when the German breakthrough and the growing defeatism of the French leaders had convinced him that their departure from France was inevitable. Yvonne de Gaulle knew that on receipt of a simple message she must leave the house as unostentatiously as possible and make her way to Brest, where she would board a ship for Britain.

Now de Gaulle arranged for the message to be sent, and set about his own last preparations. He already had a box packed in his rooms. It contained essential luggage and important papers which he must have for his work for France.

Before going to his rooms he called at the hotel where Sir Ronald Campbell, the British diplomat, was staying. "I have decided to leave for England," de Gaulle told Campbell. "Is there a plane leaving soon?"

"The plane which brought you back will be taking Sir Edward Spears back to England the day after tomorrow," the Ambassador replied. "Go to see General Spears, and I will have a word with him as well."

Spears readily fell in with the suggestion, and while de Gaulle went off to report to Reynaud, the British soldier warned the pilot of the plane that he would be taking off for London early on the following day.

Reynaud was in a despondent mood, but when de Gaulle told him that he was about to return to London the politician produced from his secret funds 100,000 francs and handed them to him. "It is little enough, but it will help you for a few days."

They shook hands, and de Gaulle went into the streets, his mind a mass of conflicting emotions. Reynaud could have been a great leader if only he had possessed a stronger will. When de Gaulle was with him the politician was firmly wedded to Gaullist theories and plans. But when others had the opportunity to exercise their wills on him he was not difficult to sway.

Spears and de Gaulle laid their plans carefully. It was decided that the fact that de Gaulle, who had been in effect the French counterpart of Spears, the British liaison with the French Government, was going to the airport to see him off would arouse no suspicions. Spears took the opportunity of picking up de Gaulle's box that evening and taking it back to his room. In the morning it would thus attract no attention when de Gaulle left for the airport.

The almost complete disorganization of French life made matters easier for them both. In the morning de Gaulle, de Courcel with him, drove in leisurely fashion to the Bordeaux airport. They arrived before Spears, drove up, and informed the airport officials that they had come officially to bid farewell to the British officer.

When Spears at last arrived the two Frenchmen chatted with him while the luggage was put aboard the plane. It included the large box. Then de Gaulle and de Courcel strolled out to the waiting aircraft with Spears. For a time they chatted by the door of the plane, while the airport men waited to pull away the gangway.

Almost at the last moment the two Generals shook hands, and Spears went up the gangway and stood in the doorway. As the gangway was pulled away the pilot of the plane shouted that he needed a rope to tie down the box, and one was hurriedly found in the airport building. De Gaulle himself took it from the man who ran out with it, threw up one end to Spears, and, as the British General pulled, jumped for the door. The next moment he

was scrambling into the plane, and as the engines roared
into full life de Courcel, with a flying leap, landed beside
him.

Seconds later they were in the air and settling down for
the flight to England. De Gaulle looked back on to the
airport, and his thoughts were of his wife and of France.
As they passed over the west-coast ports the plane was
low enough to reveal the running down of commercial
life in the country. The silent Frenchman, looking down
on the desolation, thought of his wife and his children, of
his mother, who was gravely ill in her home at Paimont, of
friends he had left behind who would soon be obeying the
orders of traitorous Frenchmen, as well as those of the
invaders. He wondered if he would see any of them again.
And then his thoughts turned to the future. With the ability he had to shut all personal worries and considerations
from his mind, he thought only of France and what he
could do to ensure that the days of her tribulation and her
shame would be short.

At Carantec Yvonne de Gaulle had received her husband's message. She had already made the necessary ar-
rangements for her own journey to safety. With her children and Mlle. Potel, and a tiny black basket as her sole
luggage, she left Carantec as if for a day's outing. They
knew that only two ships were leaving Brest for Britain
that day, one at 1:30 P.M., the other at 9 P.M. They planned
to catch the first, but their car was delayed, and they arrived only to see the ship leaving harbor.

A little over two hours later that ship had been tor-
pedoed and had sunk with the loss of all but ten people.

The family got aboard the night boat without trouble,
and before de Gaulle had left Bordeaux his wife and family
were on their way to Falmouth. Two days later they

reached England, and almost the first thing they saw was a newspaper headline, "De Gaulle Heads the Free French."

Yvonne de Gaulle, after much questioning, at last found the General's telephone number in London and put through a call. It is said that when he heard his wife's voice de Gaulle said quietly, "Ah, so you have arrived. I knew you would succeed. Take the train to London, and I will meet you at Paddington."

12

Birth of the Free French

❧ The aircraft which flew General de Gaulle to London made a landing in Jersey before finishing its flight at Croydon airport. It was therefore after noon when the General and de Courcel reached the capital. While the General booked rooms for them at the Rubens Hotel, de Courcel telephoned the French Ambassador, Charles Corbin, and informed him of their arrival. He told de Gaulle that his reception had been noticeably cool, and they had the same experience when they reported to Churchill's office and to the service missions.

De Gaulle was not unduly worried over this. He realized that the British Government had a very dangerous situation to face. There was still some possibility, however remote, of keeping France in the fight, and any hasty action towards de Gaulle which would infuriate Pétain and make capitulation certain might prejudice the whole war effort.

With typical care de Gaulle sat in his hotel room and considered all the points at issue. He was certain that France was about to surrender, and he was convinced that not a moment must be lost in minimizing the damaging effects of that capitulation. Of one thing he was convinced: on no account would France withdraw from the war and be for ever labelled as the only Allied nation to surrender. In London were the exiled Governments of Poland, Holland, and Overseas Belgium, of Norway and Denmark, of Luxembourg and Czechoslovakia, and he was determined that a recognized Government of France should stand alongside them and be accorded equal treatment with them.

His mind was soon made up, and he got in touch with Churchill without delay. Churchill cooperated to the full and without hesitation. He arranged that the B.B.C. would transmit a message from de Gaulle to the French people as soon as it was know that Pétain had asked for an armistice. In fact, while the two men were actually talking the French Prime Minister had made his request to the Germans. On the following morning de Gaulle hurried to the microphone and broadcast his message:

"The Service chiefs who for many years have been at the head of the French Army have formed a Government. That Government, alleging that our Army is defeated, have contacted the enemy to stop the fighting. But has the last word been spoken? Has hope completely disappeared? Is defeat certain? No. No.

"Believe me, for I speak with a full knowledge of everything I say, I declare that nothing is lost for France. The means that conquered us can be used to give us one day the victory.

"This war is not ended by the Battle of France. This war is a world war. Crushed to-day by mechanized forces, we shall conquer in the future with superior mechanized forces.

"For France is not alone. She is not alone. She has a vast Empire behind her. She can combine with the British Empire, which holds the seas and is continuing the struggle. She can, like England, have limitless access to the immense industrial powers of the United States.

"I, General de Gaulle, speaking from London, invite the French officers and soldiers who may be in British territory, now or at a later date, with their arms or without their arms—I invite the engineers and the workers skilled in the manufacture of armaments who may be, now or in the future, on British soil—to get in touch with me.

"Whatever may come, the flame of French resistance must never be extinguished; and it will not be extinguished."

Almost his first act after the broadcast was to transfer from the Rubens Hotel to a small three-room flat in Seymour Place, which was put at his disposal by a British friend. There he waited for his first volunteers.

He had not long to wait. De Courcel came in with a tall, lean Frenchman—M. Bouchinet-Serreulles, an engineer. The Free French forces were in being.

In France the reception of de Gaulle's speech was mixed. For a little while the people walked the streets with raised heads and straighter shoulders, and there was a good deal of playing of the "Marseillaise" from shop loudspeakers. But some newspapers, among them the Communist *L'Humanité,* supported the capitulation on the old grounds that England wished to see a continuation "of the massacre of our brothers and sons in order to enable the 40 million Englishmen to exploit the 400 millions on the Continent."

De Gaulle was not unduly surprised at this. On the following day, June 19, he again went to the B.B.C. microphone and spoke:

"In the face of the paralysis of all our institutions I, General de Gaulle, assume the right to speak in the name of France.

"In the name of France I make this formal declaration:

"Every Frenchman who is bearing arms has a sacred duty to continue resistance.

"To lay down arms, to evacuate a military position, to relinquish even the smallest slice of French land to the enemy, would be a crime against the nation.

"At the present hour I speak, above all, of French North Africa, for an intact North Africa.

"The Italian armistice is a clumsy trap.

"In the Africa of Clauzel, of Bugeaud, of Lyautey, of Noguès, every man possessing a shred of honor must refuse to carry out the conditions imposed by the enemy.

"We must not let the panic which has gripped Bordeaux spread overseas.

"Soldiers of France, wherever you may be, arise."

It was, in fact, a futile, though courageous, appeal. The almost unknown soldier could not hope to rally France at that moment of blackest despair. The French people, who had never been thrown completely into the war, were sick of its frustrations and its terrors. As the last remnants of the British Expeditionary Force were evacuated from Cherbourg the French workers helped them on their way in the belief that that would mean an end of the bombing and the terror.

In London de Gaulle waited for his volunteers. One, Georges Boris, a noncommissioned officer-interpreter who had escaped from Dunkirk, located the General at his Seymour Place flat. When Boris entered only Serreulles was there, but soon de Gaulle came in with de Courcel.

"I have come to volunteer, General," Boris said.

"Come in, monsieur. You are very welcome," answered de Gaulle, and pulled up a chair for his visitor.

"I want to tell you all that has happened in the past weeks," said the General, and proceeded to a condensed

analysis of the meetings and the conferences and the gradual collapse of French resistance.

"Now I will tell you what we plan to do," de Gaulle told
the soldier. "We shall organize all Frenchmen in this
country and in the Empire. We shall fight on every front
alongside our Allies and on equal terms with them. We
shall prepare for the day when we shall lead an army back
to France itself.

"In the meantime we shall make contact with all Frenchmen in France, arrange for those who want to join us to
come here, and organize those who wish to stay in a great
guerrilla army. In that way the enemy can be harassed on
every front, and we can spread his forces throughout
France, for he will never know when the blow will fall or
where.

"Now, M. Boris, I will tell you of the immediate pros-
pects. Britain has a magnificent Navy, but the threat will
come not from the sea, but from the air. Britain's Air
Force is excellent, but small. If it should be overcome and
the Germans can follow up and land heavy tanks there is
little on the ground to contain them. But the passive defenses of this country are excellently arranged.

"If Britain can hold out America will come into the
fight within several months, or at most a year, and all will
be well."

De Gaulle's tone throughout had been calm and matter-
of-fact. Boris has since recalled that it seemed at that
moment that the General was no longer conscious that he
was talking to a humble noncommissioned officer of the
French Army, but that he was talking to France itself.

The newly enrolled member of the Free French Forces
set to work at once at headquarters. The Army was growing.

Day by day de Gaulle built up the nucleus of a staff. It was a pitifully slow process and pitifully inadequate at the best, but he remarked to his office staff one day, "It is like building up the Fourth Division again. That came out of nothing, and so will this."

The British Government placed a car at his disposal. He was forced to look round for a driver, as he realized that he could not spare the time to drive himself, and in any case the car would have to serve for all the headquarters staff for the time being. A Frenchman volunteered for the job.

"So you'd like to drive for me, would you?" de Gaulle asked him.

"Yes, General."

"Good. You realize that you will get no thanks and even less reward. You will leave the Army with the same number of stars as you entered it—just as I shall. Others will get rewards and promotion, but not we. But if you think it is an honor to drive for me I regard it as an honor to have you."

It was in such ways that he inspired his first volunteers.

Immediately on his arrival in London on June 17 de Gaulle had telegraphed the French Government in Bordeaux advising them of his decision and offering his services in further negotiations with the British Government and the United States. The answer had been a summons to return at once to France. Now, on June 20, de Gaulle wrote personally to Weygand entreating him to put himself at the head of the Resistance, and assuring him that he would serve him faithfully. De Gaulle also tried to contact those in the Reynaud Government whom he knew had been ready to carry on the fight, and to urge them to come to Britain to join him. In his letter to Weygand, de

Gaulle ended with the words, "I send you my best respects if your answer is 'Yes.'"

There was no idea in de Gaulle's mind at that time of assuming the command of the Free French Forces. He was anxious that some other leader, who would be better known and therefore likely to be more readily acceptable to the French people, should be persuaded to take his courage in his hands and declare for continued resistance. On June 19 de Gaulle sent a cable to General Noguès, the French Commander-in-Chief, North Africa, placing himself under his orders should he reject the armistice. In the next few days de Gaulle addressed similar appeals to General Mittelhausser, Commander-in-Chief, Levant; to Gabriel Puaux, the High Commissioner in the Lebanon; to his old friend General Catroux, Governor-General in Indo-China; and to Marcel Peyrouton, Resident-General in Tunisia.

Catroux, through his son, then in London, gave his support to de Gaulle. But Noguès, who had at first supported continued resistance, hesitated when he learned that the majority of French leaders and commanders overseas had accepted Pétain's orders, and himself gave way. General Legentilhomme, Commander-in-Chief in Somaliland, declared for de Gaulle.

De Gaulle, solitary in his flat in Seymour Place, had to face the fact that almost every hand was against him. He had installed his wife and children in a small house in Richmond, and he was able to see them at weekends only. The rest of the week he worked without respite. Gradually men were coming to see him to join his Free French Forces, but it was a pitifully small number, and a man less determined than de Gaulle would have been disheartened.

He knew that the attitude of the British Government

was one of caution, and he was not at any time disposed to blame them for that, even though he did his utmost to see that the cause of France was not overlooked. Churchill, with the knowledge that a majority of the French forces in Britain, after the Norway and Dunkirk evacuations, wished to return home, and realizing that the most important forces now available to France not yet under German control were ships of the Navy commanded by Darlan, wished to know whether there was still a chance to bring them over to the Allies.

It was in those first days in London that the attitude of de Gaulle, so far as the conduct of the war was concerned, crystallized and hardened. From that moment, more than ever, his first considerations were always for France. The common effort of the Allies came second.

The signing of the armistice on June 22 was a bitter moment for de Gaulle. He declared: "To-night I shall say simply, because some one must say it, that unspeakable shame and revolt rise in the hearts of all good Frenchmen. . . . France is like a boxer floored by a terrific punch. She is down for the count. But she knows, she feels, that life still beats strong and deep within her. She knows, she feels, that the fight is not over, that the cause is not given up.

"She knows, she feels, that she deserves a great deal better than the slavery accepted by the Government of Bordeaux.

"She knows, she feels, that in her Empire powerful forces of resistance stand ready to save her honor. Already the will to continue the war has been revealed at many points in French overseas territories.

"She knows, she feels, that her Allies are more than ever resolved to fight and conquer.

"She sees in the New World enormous material and moral strength which perhaps will arise one day to crush the enemies of liberty.

"We must have an ideal, we must have hope. Somewhere the flame of French resistance must glimmer and burst into fire. . . . One day, I give you my promise, our forces—a picked French Army, a mechanized land, sea, and air force—in common action with our Allies, will restore liberty to the world and greatness to France."

When that declaration was made the forces of Free France numbered fewer than two hundred men.

A day later de Gaulle was stripped of his rank by the Pétain Government.

It was a strange and unreal period. The French Government still acted through its Ambassador, Charles Corbin, but de Gaulle was a regular visitor to the Embassy. "I am too old a civil servant to act other than on the orders of the Government," Corbin told de Gaulle.

The British Government hindered de Gaulle's approaches to the servicemen of France in their camps in England. But the General was able to visit the Light Alpine Division, which had fought in Norway under the command of General Béthouart, who, though he supported de Gaulle's stand, declared that the majority of his men wanted to return to France, and he felt that he must go with them.

De Gaulle saw the 13th Foreign Legion, commanded by Lieutenant-Colonel Magrin-Verneret, with Captain Koenig (later to command at Bir Hacheim in one of the finest engagements of the North African fighting) as the adjutant; 200 Chasseurs Alpins, some tanks, artillery, engineers, signals, several General Staff officers, including Commandant Conchard and Captains Dewavrin and Tissier; the naval officers Captains d'Argenkieu, Wietzel, Mou-

lec, and Jourden; the submarine commanders Cabanier
and Drogou, and the armed-trawler captain Deschatres.
These were few enough on which to build a resistance to
the Germans.

The Americans were completely indifferent to de Gaulle,
and to a great extent Roosevelt never changed this attitude to the Frenchman. Churchill, at the outset, looked
upon de Gaulle as a courageous idealist; Roosevelt always
regarded him as a nuisance and an embarrassment. Both
sought actively for an alternative to the tall Frenchman—
Catroux, Darlan, Giraud, all being considered. But no one
came forward, and possibly this fact had some bearing
on the decision taken by the British Government on June
28 publicly to recognize de Gaulle as Leader of Free
France.

This enabled de Gaulle to announce that he would take
under his authority "all Frenchmen who remain on British
territory or who come there in future; a French land, sea,
and air force will be formed immediately." De Gaulle also
declared, "There is here created a French organization for
the manufacture and purchase of armaments and a French
organization for research into the improvement of war
matériel."

He appealed: "Generals, higher commanders, governors
of the colonies, communicate with me so that we may
unite our efforts and save French territories. In spite of
the capitulations already made by so many responsible for
the honor of the flag and the greatness of the nation, Free
France has not ceased to exist. We shall prove it by arms."

De Gaulle had now transferred his headquarters to St.
Stephen's House on London's Victoria Embankment. There
the stream of volunteers gradually increased, until he
could number his followers in thousands.

At 10 P.M. on June 30 an important visitor presented

himself. It was Vice-Admiral Muselier, who had escaped from France by way of Gibraltar, where he had managed to enroll some units of the fleet and some airmen under the banner of the Free French.

De Gaulle congratulated Muselier on his escape from France and on the manner in which he had rallied the Free French in Gibraltar. He asked the Admiral if he had news of his family, and mentioned that he had his own in England, that his son Philippe wished to join the Free French Navy. He mentioned that he himself now had ample funds provided by the British Government, and that he proposed that Muselier should take some, which the Admiral refused. Then abruptly, as if he had been sparring for an opening, de Gaulle brought the interview to an end. "Good, it is agreed that you shall command the Navy and Air Force in the legion I am organizing. Get yourself into uniform, and we shall talk longer to-morrow."

An official order signed by de Gaulle was issued on the following day naming Muselier commander of the Free French Navy and Air Force.

Now there was a great rallying of Frenchmen to the Free French. De Gaulle organized a Cabinet of his associates. De Courcel was *chef de cabinet*. René Pleven and Denis were to look after the all-important matter of finance. Antoine would deal with civil problems, and René Cassin all legal matters. Maurice Schumann was to work on radio propaganda. Roger Massip took charge of information and Bingen naval matters. Tissier, Dewavrin, and d'Hettier de Boislambert formed de Gaulle's Staff.

Behind the scenes in the British Admiralty there was great activity, which was kept carefully concealed from de Gaulle. Convinced at last that the French fleet was not to be sent over to the Allied side, Churchill sent a message on July 3 to Admiral Somerville at Gibraltar: "You are charged with a mission which is the most unpleasant and the most difficult that any British Admiral has ever had to fulfill, but we have the utmost confidence in you and know that you will execute it rigorously."

An ultimatum was sent to Admiral Gensoul, commanding the French squadron at Mars-el-Kebir and Oran. It said that he could carry on the war with Britain, make for a British port with his ships, or seek asylum in a port of the West Indies under the control of the Americans. If none of these was acceptable an order would be given in six hours to sink the ships.

When no answer was received a further message was sent to Gensoul: "Either accept our conditions, or scuttle your ships, or we shall bombard you before nightfall."

Gensoul gave an assurance that in no case would he ever allow the ships of France to fall into the hands of the Germans or Italians, but in the early evening the British attack started, and ten minutes later aircraft had sunk the "Bretagne," "Provence," and "Dunkerque," and only the "Strasbourg" managed to escape to Toulon.

Meanwhile in Portsmouth and Plymouth and other British ports where French ships were anchored British troops were sent to arrest the officers and crews. There was some fighting before this was done, although Muselier, at Dartmouth and Portsmouth, managed to persuade some of the officers and men to throw in their lot with the Free French Forces, while others agreed to join the Royal Navy.

At St. Stephen's House the news was received with consternation. For a moment or so de Gaulle was beside himself with rage. When that abated a little all that he could think of was the damaging blow to Anglo-French relations just as the accord was bringing more and more Frenchmen to his side. But when his anger cooled even more he set about the task of examining the whole question in the light of Allied needs. He could see that the French fleet, if it had been brought over to the German side, could have been an important factor in the immediate struggle.

He showed once more his greatness when he issued a declaration on July 8 which ran:

> A particularly cruel episode took place on July 3. I shall speak of it plainly, straightforwardly, for in a drama in which each people is playing for its life, men of goodwill must have the courage to look circumstances in the face. . . . First of all, there is not a single Frenchman who did not feel grief and anger when he learned that the ships of the French fleet had been sunk by our Allies. . . . To the French I ask them to consider the whole situation from the only point of view that can count in the final analysis—I mean from the point of view of ultimate victory and liberation. By virtue of a dishonorable obligation the Government in Bordeaux had agreed to place our ships at the disposal of the enemy. There is not the slightest doubt that through both principle and necessity the enemy would have used them, either against England or against our own Empire. Without beating about the bush, I say it was better for them to be destroyed. . . . Thoughtful Englishmen cannot fail to see that no victory would be possible for them if the soul of France ever went over to the enemy. Frenchmen worthy of the name must recognize that an English defeat would seal forever their subjugation. Whatever happens, even though one of the two is temporarily under the yoke of the common enemy, our two great peoples will remain bound to each other. They will win together or they will both succumb.

Despite this interpretation of the incident, the effect on the French in Britain and overseas who had thoughts of rallying to the fight was disastrous. Immediately the recruiting rate fell, and a great many people who had promised to come forward in fact never appeared. In France the Vichy Government exploited the situation to the full.

13

The Failure at Dakar

❦ Soon after the surprising incident of Mars-el-Kebir de Gaulle set up his Deuxième Bureau, and entrusted the running of this to Captain Dewavrin, who had adopted the name of Passy. Muselier, who was already showing signs of restiveness, was of the opinion that the men who were forming this nucleus of the Intelligence Service were all too young and inexperienced. He advised the appointment of a trained and experienced officer of the Navy to take charge of the Intelligence Service. De Gaulle's reply was brusque. "The Navy should keep to its ships," he said. "It is forbidden to meddle in what does not concern it."

In forming his Intelligence Service de Gaulle had several objects. He was intent on beginning his infiltration of France at the earliest opportunity, and his old love of reconnaissance persuaded him that this was essential if the Allies were ever to cross the water barrier between England and France. He also wished to be kept informed, so far as possible, of all that was going on around him. One thing the incident at Mars-el-Kebir had taught him was that he could not always rely on his Allies to keep him informed of their plans. On several occasions before the end of the war there were to be decisions affecting France and her Empire which were never referred to de Gaulle.

But his Deuxième Bureau, once it got into its stride, was

more successful than many people gave it credit for. It was able to keep de Gaulle advised of many things which his Allies wished to keep from him.

De Gaulle was working on the over-all plan for the war, and he at no time allowed Churchill to imagine that the forces of Free France could be given any less consideration than those of the other exiled Governments.

In June 1940 de Gaulle was working in his room with Warrant Officer Boris. Suddenly the sound of the nightly German reconnaissance plane could be heard passing overhead. De Gaulle got up from his desk and walked to the huge map of Europe, the Middle East, and Asia which almost covered the wall.

"That is our greatest danger at the moment," he said. "We are surrounded by German air bases." His finger stabbed out at the map—Norway, Denmark, Germany, the Netherlands, Belgium, France. "It is essential for us to combat this half-circle of offensive bases by forming our own half-circle," said the General. He jabbed his finger at Morocco. "Here, and here," moving along the North African coastline to Algeria, through Tunisia, Libya, Egypt, and then up through Palestine, he continued to poke his finger on the map, saying, "And here, and here." His hand continued up through the Lebanon and Turkey and on into Russia, where it paused.

"But, General, you are pointing to Russia! Have you forgotten that she is on the side of Germany?" Boris exclaimed.

"No, I have not forgotten. But can you believe that it will be many months before Russia is attacked by Hitler and she is in the war on our side?" de Gaulle said, and returned once more to his desk.

The first Free French units were now in training, and

some, the airmen, were already in actual combat. De Gaulle had adopted as his insignia the Cross of Lorraine. There were now 7,000 men serving under that flag.

But he had to be constantly on the lookout that the interests of France were being studied and respected. Sometimes it was only a little thing that worried him, but often it had great importance. He was careful never to miss an opportunity of drawing attention to the rights and privileges of the Free French as a full and equal partner in the struggle, and this soon earned him a name for being difficult to work with. Thus at a meeting on July 12, when the question of deciding once and for all what the officers and men of the French Navy intended to do—return to France, decide to fight with the Free French, or join the Royal Navy—came up for discussion, de Gaulle pointed out to Admiral Dickens that the British suggestion of visiting the camp at Liverpool where French Navy men were collected and presenting every man with a brochure explaining the conditions offered by Britain had never been brought to his notice, nor had he been told of the proposed brochure. He insisted that his staff should be allowed to assist in the preparation of the pamphlet. It was a small incident, but de Gaulle attached importance to it.

With the end of July it became obvious to every one that the leaders of France—the politicians who had been in office in the last days of the fighting—were not succeeding in escaping to Britain to carry on the struggle. Reynaud, Mandel, Marin, Herriot, Blum, Campinchi, Monnet, all had been expected, but none had arrived.

In the first week in August the British Government and de Gaulle reached an agreement on the organization, utilization, and conditions of service of the Free French Forces.

Churchill described de Gaulle as "recognized by His Majesty's Government in the United Kingdom as head of all Free Frenchmen, wherever located, who rally round you for the defense of the Allied cause." Churchill added, "I take this occasion to declare that His Majesty's Government is determined, when the Allied arms shall have won the victory, to insure the complete restoration of the independence and greatness of France."

De Gaulle felt no great elation over the unique tribute to his character and integrity. A single Frenchman had become accredited to a foreign Government without ever having been a member of his own Parliament, without ever having received a vote of confidence of his own people. His extraordinary single-mindedness allowed him to go steadily ahead with his plans as if the situation was completely normal.

He did show some emotion—in private—on August 23, when at Aldershot King George VI reviewed the Free French "Army" with de Gaulle by his side. That tribute, more, perhaps, even than the support he had received from a great many private citizens, some of whom sent their wedding rings as contributions to the French cause, made de Gaulle feel that he was at last beginning to win real recognition for his little force of volunteers. Among the other Governments in exile in London he was still regarded more as a joke than as a man representing a resurgence of French fighting spirit. Only Sikorski, of the Polish Government, and Beneš of Czechoslovakia gave him the fullest cooperation.

De Gaulle had hoped that France would continue the fight from Africa, and he lost no time in setting in motion his plans. But now his task was very different from what it would have been had there been no armistice which left

part of France itself and all of the overseas territories outside the occupation. Though he sent constant messages to
the leaders of the French communities all along North
Africa and in the Levant, he soon found that enthusiasm
for the Allied cause had waned somewhat. An armistice
which on paper had taken control of all French territories
could have fired a revolt. But in North Africa it was the
status quo.

He finally sent Pleven, de Parant, d'Hettier de Boislambert, Larminat, and Leclerc to the French colonies as
emissaries. Soon they were able to report that the Chads,
the Cameroons, and most of French Equatorial Africa had
come over to Free France. Only Dakar and the Gabon
continued to support Vichy.

De Gaulle decided that it was impossible to mobilize
French Africa to the side of the Free French so long as
Dakar and the rest of Senegal remained faithful to Pétain.
But he knew only too well how strongly defended the port
could be, and he did not wish to repeat the vast mistake
of Mars-el-Kebir and to have any hand in the shedding of
French blood at a time when the rest of the French African
possessions were rallying to his flag.

The division of responsibility between de Gaulle and his
aides and Churchill and his, which made for misunder-
standing, a momentary aberration on the part of de Gaulle,
which involved him in unusual equivocation, and a slow-
ness of organization all contributed to the failure of the
enterprise which followed and to the need for very much
greater efforts in the future to win North Africa for the
Allies.

De Gaulle's first plan was to land a force of French
troops at Conakry, in French Guinea, and to carry them
overland through Guinea to the railroad which links Ba-

mako, in French Sudan, with Dakar, the principal city in Senegal, and the capital of French West Africa. He reckoned that the news of a French column marching on the capital of French West Africa would bring over the waverers in Senegal to his side.

It was not the most brilliant of de Gaulle's military plans. It relied almost entirely on the provision of sufficient vessels to transport his troops and supplies, and a supply line through the undeveloped, almost roadless land areas once they had landed. De Gaulle had had no experience of African conditions at that time. He was committing what for him would normally have been an unthinkable error in planning a campaign on insufficient premises. And unfortunately his assistants had no better experience of Africa.

Muselier, in fact, had advised a more direct approach to Dakar. The Admiral wanted a fast naval force to land troops at Port Etienne, in Mauretania, and from there cut the lines of communication of Dakar with Algeria and Morocco. When that was accomplished a naval force would present itself outside Dakar and call for the authorities to join Free France, suggested Muselier.

De Gaulle liked this suggestion at the outset, but Churchill declared that, although the British Government would support the plan, it could not spare a considerable naval force for long. Therefore the operation must be carried out as a direct approach to the port, with an unarmed boat carrying ashore representatives of Free France to parley with the authorities ashore. These men would make it plain that if the Governor of Senegal allowed de Gaulle's forces to land the fleet would immediately be withdrawn. While these parleys were going on aircraft would be flying overhead and distributing messages of friendship in the form of leaflets.

De Gaulle realized that he could not carry out any plan for winning Senegal to the side of the Free French without the support both of the British Navy and of the Royal Air Force as well. He realized, too, that the British leader and his Admiralty advisers had now themselves decided that Dakar, lying as it did along the Cape route of the supply lines to Egypt, could, if it fell into the hands of the German fleet, constitute a real menace to Britain's sea routes. Thus, even if he withdrew from the project at Dakar, he knew that the British would go on with it. In that case there would have been much more danger of full-scale war, in which many French lives and a great deal of French property would be destroyed, with consequent propaganda value for Vichy France.

The Free French leader accepted the plan as outlined by Churchill. But the business of assembling the ships and of preparing the troops took so long that the D-day suggested, September 7, was passed. De Gaulle knew from his intelligence reports from France that preparations were going on in Toulon for a large-scale reinforcement of Dakar. This reinforcement, in fact, arrived on September 22, one day before the British fleet, with de Gaulle on board, arrived off the port. Moreover, there was never any doubt that the Vichy Government was always fully informed not only of the plan, but of the actual date it would be put into operation.

The whole affair exploded in fire and slaughter. After de Gaulle had requested that the expedition be cancelled Churchill himself ordered a re-engagement. There were casualties on both sides, and the action was finally called off. It had been most damaging to the prestige of de Gaulle himself, because it was attributed to him, to the Free French, because it had failed, and also, in somewhat less a degree, to Britain, because Britain had taken a leading role in it.

De Gaulle might then have been prepared to carry out his idea to land at Conakry and to thrust northward into Senegal. But the British Navy was not accommodating, and Admiral Cunningham instead escorted de Gaulle southward to Douala, in the Cameroons, where he disembarked with the troops with which he had hoped to occupy Dakar.

It seemed that the whole world was laughing at de Gaulle. In America he was the butt of every crude joke possible. In Britain the whole affair was dismissed as an "absurd adventure." De Gaulle, inwardly grieved to an extent that he could not remember for many months, landed in the Cameroons. The enthusiasm of his reception was like a salve to his distress. With a display of self-control he never at any moment mentioned the mistakes of Dakar; never made one allegation of lack of good faith against Britain. Instead he utilized the resistance at Dakar as a means of stirring up even greater fervor for the Free French cause.

Churchill went on record in the House of Commons that nothing which had happened in any way lessened the confidence the British Government had in de Gaulle. Yet at the same time there was a tendency among many people to demand that Catroux, recently arrived in London, might be given the command of the Free French in place of de Gaulle. Churchill certainly thought that there was some point in this, but not because he wished to indulge in the classic maneuver of divide and rule, but because the idea of cooperating with de Gaulle was something that Washington was not prepared to envisage, and Churchill was not prepared to balk Washington on this point.

Even before the Dakar incident Churchill had delegated Catroux to go to Cairo and there await action in the Levant. De Gaulle had immediately replied that although he thought the idea a good one, he felt that the decision was one which required his agreement, as head of all the Free French Forces, in accordance with the agreement signed on August 7.

Catroux settled all question of the leadership of the Free French by travelling to Fort Lamy, in the Chad, for the special purpose of presenting a report to de Gaulle and assuring him of his loyalty and support.

Behind all this apparent intrigue on the part of the Allies were constant differences of opinion and constant hints that all was not well with the Free French organization. In it there were still men who felt that de Gaulle was not the natural leader of all Fighting France. There were many who suspected his motives, particularly those who held Left-wing views.

De Gaulle's attitude of reserve and unbending will had already begun to build up the story of the "De Gaulle Myth" and suspicions that he felt that he could do no wrong. In London also there was a direct conflict of opinion between Muselier, de Gaulle's second-in-command, and Commandant Fontaine, who directed the merchant marine of Free France. All these things contributed to a feeling on the part of the other Allied leaders that perhaps de Gaulle was not the man they had thought him, and that they should not completely close the door to a possible replacement.

Meanwhile in Equatorial Africa de Gaulle, with Larminat, organized the operations in the Gabon. Attacks were made on Lambaréné, Mitzic, and Libreville. Churchill had agreed that certain units of the Royal Navy should lie

ready off Libreville, and take no action unless absolutely
necessary. They were not required.

Mitzic and Lambarène were taken on October 27, and
Libreville, where Leclerc and Koenig were engaged, surrendered on November 9. The Gabon was taken with the
loss of twenty killed, for Port Gentil surrendered on
November 12 without fighting.

This brought all French Equatorial Africa under Free
French control. It meant also that there was a Free French
line of communication right through Central Africa to the
Libyan Desert, and a spearhead threatening the Axis lines
of communication from Tripoli to the East.

On October 27 de Gaulle had a statement issued from
Brazzaville:

> France is going through one of the most terrible crises of her
> history. Her frontiers, her Empire, her independence, and even
> her soul are menaced with destruction.
>
> There no longer exists a real Government of France.
>
> The organization with its seat at Vichy which pretends to carry
> the name of the French Government is unconstitutional and has
> submitted to the invader. In this state of servitude the Pétain
> organization cannot be a Government, and in effect it is only an
> instrument used by the enemies of France against the honor and
> interests of the country.
>
> It is necessary, then, that a new power should assume charge
> of the direction of the French war effort. Events have imposed
> on me that sacred duty. I will not fail it.
>
> I will exercise my powers in the name of France and solely to
> defend it, and I make this solemn promise that I will render an
> account of my actions to the representatives of the French people
> as soon as it is possible to do so freely.
>
> To assist me in my task I now bring into being as from to-day
> an Empire Defense Council.
>
> Officers, soldiers, and citizens of France, at this very moment
> infamous or senile leaders are trying to hand over our Empire to
> the enemy.
>
> Arise! To arms!

His Brazzaville statement was intended not only to convince the waverers in Equatorial Africa, but to draw the attention of the people of Senegal and farther north that a new French Government had been installed in Africa and was prepared to carry the fight into the occupied territories.

14

Troubles with Admiral Muselier

❧ De Gaulle had left behind him in London a triumvirate to administer the Free French Forces while he was away in Africa. He had named Muselier as senior commander of the Free French military forces in Great Britain; Fontaine (whose real name was Antoine, and who had been connected with the Metropolitain of Paris and of the Compagnies françaises d'électricité) as chief of the Civil Service; and Dewavrin (Passy) as Chief of Staff.

This arrangement did not suit Muselier at all. He addressed a note of protest to de Gaulle, pointing out that the division of responsibility would weaken the organization. The Admiral was also, perhaps justifiably, annoyed that important messages from the General would go direct to Fontaine or Passy, without first passing through his hands. In that way the Commander-in-Chief in Britain would be denied knowledge of affairs which might have the greatest importance for Free France.

De Gaulle had decided that both Passy and Serreulles should correspond direct with him, and very soon by this means the General had word of trouble between Fontaine and André Labarthe, who had been one of the first to join the Free French movement, and who was director of the armament supply service and of scientific research.

In due course this was to result in the removal of Labarthe from his position.

Muselier felt that he had been slighted, and his pride was certainly severely wounded. He demanded of de Gaulle the right to promote officers of the naval forces— a right which he felt was essential in view of the rapid build-up of the force.

The Admiral wrote to Churchill on September 21, while de Gaulle was still at sea on the Dakar expedition, in connection with the compensation for injury and death caused to French sailors during the Mars-el-Kebir battle. Muselier suggested that those injured and the dependents of those killed should be given a cash payment and pension. He also suggested that the British Government should promise to replace all the ships sunk as soon as the war had been won.

Churchill's view was that it was not for the British Government to make any public declaration at that moment. He expressed his sorrow, however, that the exigencies of the situation had forced the British Navy to kill and wound their French comrades, and he was sure that one day the British Government would be able to compensate those who had suffered through having obeyed blindly the orders of a superior authority which had been ill-inspired in ordering the French ships to open fire on the British.

De Gaulle, hearing of this intervention by Muselier, was angry, but for the moment took no further action. At this time Passy was organizing his Security Service, and a Captain Howard (whose real name was Meffre) was put in charge of this. Howard at once set out to investigate the loyalties of almost every one of the General's closest advisers. Muselier immediately worked for his dismissal.

News of all these intrigues reached de Gaulle in Equatorial
Africa, and he cabled Muselier in the sharpest terms, en-
joining him not to provoke discontent among the headquarters staff. He also sharply reprimanded him for carrying out promotions of officers in direct contradiction of his
own orders. Muselier replied tartly that the Navy had kept
out of all the intrigues which were racking the movement.

Information had reached de Gaulle in Africa, however,
which alleged that Muselier was in touch with Vichy
French sources, and was suggesting that Catroux, then in
London, was very much more popular with the public than
de Gaulle, and was likely to replace him. These stories,
combined with the knowledge de Gaulle already had that
Churchill himself had some thoughts on the possible value
of a change of leadership, persuaded the General that
there might be some truth in the allegations against
Muselier.

De Gaulle returned to London on November 25, filled
with doubts on what might be his best course to take with
Muselier. The Admiral's energy, even when it was directed
in criticism of de Gaulle, impressed the General greatly.
"I am anxious that your qualities of organization and command should be used in the service of France, but it is
essential that you should exercise some discipline over your
tongue and your actions," de Gaulle told the Admiral.

On December 31 Muselier took to de Gaulle several
complaints affecting members of the Free French Forces,
particularly as regards Fontaine and Howard. De Gaulle
took note of them without comment. Almost at once he
left London for a weekend in the country with his wife and
children, but during the same evening received news that
Muselier had again been taking the limelight while on a

visit to Windsor for a charity show, taking a bow when
recognized by the audience.

On January 2, 1941, at his flat in Hallam Street, St.
Marylebone, Muselier was arrested by Captain Stephens,
R.N., and two Scotland Yard inspectors, and later taken
to Pentonville Prison. From there, after two nights in a
cell, he was removed, on the intervention of the Admiralty
and the Home Secretary, to Brixton Prison. The following
day the Admiral was visited by Captain Auboyneau, of
Muselier's staff, Serreulles, of de Gaulle's personal staff,
and Major Younger, of the British Intelligence Service.
They informed the Admiral that de Gaulle was coming to
see him as soon as possible, and in any case was doing
his utmost to arrange his release.

De Gaulle was still averse to accepting the allegations,
but he could not but remember that Muselier had all along
shown some resentment of both his command and his
direction. And, apparently, the British Government had
strong evidence to back up their charges. De Gaulle therefore went carefully into the whole matter before taking
further steps. If Muselier was indeed a traitor to Free
France, de Gaulle thought that the less that was said and
done in his defense the better. If, on the other hand,
Muselier was innocent the more care taken to ensure that
the matter was kept quiet the less harm it would do to the
cause.

It was therefore not before Monday, January 6, at Scotland Yard, that de Gaulle saw his Admiral. Immediately
prior to this Muselier was shown the evidence against him
—a letter concerning the expedition to Dakar from the
Vichy French Consulate in London, supposedly signed by
General Rozoy. The letter mentioned Muselier by name.

Muselier immediately named it as false. Rozoy would

never have used official notepaper, signed his own name, or mentioned to whom he was writing in a matter as dangerous as this, Muselier argued, and in this was supported by a Scotland Yard detective.

There was also a letter dated August 11 in which a sum of £2,000 was mentioned as payment to Muselier for putting obstacles in the way of naval recruitment for the Free French Forces. A third letter, dated September 17, gave the news that Catroux was in London, was more popular than de Gaulle, and might yet be chosen as his successor. And a fourth letter, dated September 26, referred to the means by which the French submarine "Surcouf" might be got back under the control of the Vichy Government.

Muselier declared that all these letters were forgeries, and said that an examination of the signatures and of the typewriting would prove them so. He was then led into a room where de Gaulle awaited him.

The General was cold and short with his Admiral. He assured Muselier that he would soon be free again, and that he was personally seeing to it that matters were hurried. But he left him in little doubt that he regarded him as having brought much of this trouble on himself, and therefore, in the outcome, had caused more trouble to the Free French Forces. De Gaulle informed Muselier that Captain Colin, Howard's assistant, would be charged with having forged the letters.

There were for de Gaulle some good results of all this disturbance in his organization. The British Government, recognizing that it had made a serious error, went out of its way to show its regrets not only to Muselier, but also to the Free French. Thus, while Muselier received a letter of deep regret from Anthony Eden and an admission of error, de Gaulle was able to clear up several points of importance which had been held up for overlong. He was able to reach agreement on the question of Free French military courts which would operate in conformity with British military law; the exchange value of the franc—fixed at 176.25 to the pound; and the establishment of a Free French Bank.

Muselier, lunched at Downing Street by Churchill and received at Buckingham Palace by the King, was left with a bitter resentment against de Gaulle, whom he constantly accused of not dismissing Howard in the face of repeated proofs of the man's perfidy and of promises of action. In addition, Muselier took to more open criticism of his leader's politics and decisions.

De Gaulle, however, had a great admiration for Muselier's gifts as a naval commander and organizer, and he had no intention of allowing personal considerations, which the Admiral appeared anxious to keep in the forefront, to react against the best interests of Free France.

It was essential at this time that de Gaulle should have the greatest measure of unity in the Free French Forces. He was in process of organizing the first units from Britain of the French Resistance, and had to be careful that those he chose would be men who would be acceptable to the possible Underground fighters in France. He was working very hard, getting to Carlton Gardens, to which he had transferred from Seymour Place, at 9:30 A.M. and working solidly throughout the day until late at night, except for a short break for lunch in a private room at the Connaught Hotel. His only relaxation after lunch was the walk back to his office with his aides, and then he chatted on every conceivable subject. He would joke freely and laugh a great deal.

In his office he showed that he was not a good office organizer, for he was too impatient to allow a job to be finished before he handed out another. Only during his daily silent periods, when he gave himself up to thought, were his assistants ever really able to get on with their work without interruption. But soon out from the General's office would be coming a stream of directives, all written in his own hand and all meticulously subedited.

His assistants found that his phenomenal memory never deserted him, and he was capable of repeating almost verbatim the discussions and decisions of every meeting.

If his closest assistants had one fault to find with him it was that he had a habit of not always telling them every-thing that was going on. That, indeed, was also the com-plaint Muselier had against him. But it is part of de Gaulle's political understanding. He has always been fond of a joke in the form of a French political recipe: "Take from the party basket a political 'truth,' raise it to your nose, smell it carefully, make sure it is fresh, turn it over several times to see what is hiding behind it; then take a little bite, taste it prudently, start to chew it very slowly and carefully, swallow a bit, then wait and see if there is no pain and convulsions, no cold sweat. Eat little by little, taking your time and chewing every morsel. But remem-ber, always be ready to spit it out. Democracy is the right to spit it out."

This was the method of his silent periods. There can be no doubt that it was this cautious approach which made it possible for de Gaulle to work with Churchill during the war without major differences; with many others who, like de Gaulle and Churchill themselves, were natural autocrats, and with some, like Muselier, who were anxious for power.

At no time during this period of the war was de Gaulle sure that he could rely on the full cooperation of the British Government. Churchill was so completely concerned with the British battle for survival and victory that he could not give too much time to prosecute the battle of Free France with equal vigor. The overt intrigues and machinations of many members of the Free French Forces made some members of the British Government skeptical of de Gaulle's chances of ultimate success.

Thus, while de Gaulle was recruiting secret agents who would be dropped into France or put ashore from boats to build up a resistance there, the British Secret Service was organizing the same sort of thing under the title of Special Operations Executive. When de Gaulle's agents contacted likely men in France it was to find on some occasions that they had already been contacted by British agents and were enrolled in the British-directed Underground. "Britain and Free France are one and the same thing," the Frenchmen were told.

One of the first of the secret agents sent to France by de Gaulle was a naval officer, Captain Henri-Honoré d'Estienne d'Orves, who had been made chief of the Deuxième Bureau. Muselier had reluctantly parted with this officer, and he protested vehemently when it was decided that d'Estienne d'Orves should be sent to France. "He has none of the qualities necessary to the successful agent," he declared. "And in any case the chief of a Secret Service organization should not be sent out to spy."

De Gaulle agreed with these contentions, and withdrew his permission for d'Estienne d'Orves to go to France, but the naval captain pleaded with such eloquence to be allowed to undertake the first mission that de Gaulle finally gave way. In the event, d'Estienne d'Orves was betrayed' to the Germans soon after landing and was shot at Vincennes.

But there were already many others to follow him—Duclos, Fourcault, the famous Remy, Weil, Curiel, Robert, Monnier.

De Gaulle made the utmost use of the radio to get his message to France. He had none of Churchill's microphone skill but he conveyed an honesty of purpose which appealed to his growing circle of listeners. He himself appeared before the microphone once a week, but it was Maurice Schumann who most often presented the Free French case. When de Gaulle came to the microphone it was to talk of France, her greatness and her past, and the certainty of greatness in the future.

Thus on December 31, 1940, he broadcast to the French people a message for New Year's Day calling for a self-imposed curfew of one hour—the Hour of Hope. "This will be the meaning of the Hour of Hope on January 1, during which time no true Frenchman will be seen out of doors. Our provinces belong to us, our land belongs to us. Whoever seizes our provinces feeds himself on wheat grown on our soil and holds our fellow-countrymen prisoners. That man is our enemy," he said.

"France expects nothing from her enemy save this—that he should go. That he take himself off, defeated. The enemy entered our country by force of arms. The day will come when he will be driven out by force of arms. He laughs longest who laughs last.

"That is the message all Frenchmen will convey to the enemy by observing the Hour of Hope."

It was reported that not many Frenchmen obeyed the suggestion of staying indoors for the Hour of Hope, but de Gaulle had plenty of evidence that his message had set people agog. Soon he had adopted a slogan with which he ended all his broadcast messages—"France with us." This became a catch phrase in France itself.

Gradually the messages came percolating back through the Underground and across the Channel to London that the name of de Gaulle was beginning to be talked about among the men-in-the-street in France; that the activities of the Free French, now increasingly linked with de Gaulle, were stirring pride in the hearts of some Frenchmen again. There were still puzzled requests from some sources— "Who is de Gaulle?"—indicating his fantastic achievement in rallying Frenchmen at all. The over-all success was still small, however.

There could be no doubt either that the intrigues and discords among the headquarters staffs in Carlton Gardens were being reported back to France. Muselier's overt suspicions of de Gaulle's good intentions were well known in Paris, and Left-wing leaders there were for long in doubt as to whether de Gaulle was not, in fact, a dictator. Blum himself managed to get a letter to Carlton Gardens addressed to one of de Gaulle's closest advisers to ask just that question. "I know de Gaulle as a brilliant soldier," he wrote, "but can anyone now assure me that he has not now become a dictator? I know I can trust your word." Blum was assured that de Gaulle was no dictator.

These were difficulties that beset de Gaulle at every turn. Certainly he many times nearly brought himself to the point of dispensing with the help of his intractable second-in-command.

In the early months of 1941 de Gaulle was planning the operations in the Middle East, and therefore did not dismiss Muselier. As far back as September 1940 Muselier had led a mission to Alexandria to examine nearer the spot the possibilities of carrying out a *coup d'état* in Syria. The Admiral was of the opinion that action should be taken at once, as every day wasted made the chances of success more slender. With characteristic candor Muselier, in a note to the British Government, washed his hands of all responsibility for failure owing to the delays in carrying out the operation. Nor could he resist laying at the door of de Gaulle the major blame for the lack of initiative shown.

Muselier at no time appeared to have had an appreciation of the situation in the Western Desert, where the British Army, having only a poorly armed Sixth Australian Division and an ill-equipped Seventh Armored Division (the famous Desert Rats) to carry out its lightning thrusts, was engaged under Wavell in decimating an Italian Army many times its numbers. In this effort a small Free French unit under Captain Folliot was engaged at Sidi Barrani. Farther south, in Eritrea and Ethiopia, larger French forces under Colonel Monclar were engaged with the British and South Africans in the battles with the Duke of Aosta.

De Gaulle's decision to concentrate at that time on clearing the coasts of the Red Sea and of the Egyptian and Libyan areas of the enemy was amply justified by future events, for Syria and the Lebanon were never to play a major part in the conflict. But a hostile French Somaliland and Eritrea might have led to a dangerous enemy concentration across the only line of communication of the Allies between Britain, South Africa, and Egypt.

The lightning and surprising success of General Wavell's drive against the Italian Army in the Western Desert led de Gaulle to order further Free French operations at Kufra Oasis, the religious center of the Senussi, far into the desert south of Derna, in Libya, and in the Fezzan, in the south of Tripoli. These were both objects of great strategic importance, for they would make it possible to harry the lines of communication of the Axis from Tripoli to the east. The sudden reversal of fortunes brought about by the Rommel thrusts with his Afrika Corps made these plans abortive, but it in no way made greater sense of Muselier's contentions. Kufra Oasis was captured on March 4, 1941, with more than three hundred prisoners, and the Senussi were brought more certainly behind the Allied cause.

It seemed to de Gaulle at that time that it would take all the resolution of the British Commonwealth peoples to hold out in the face of the tremendous reverses they were suffering. Occasionally he had moments of despair in his Carlton Gardens office, when he would say to his aides, "I wonder if we are doing right?" But these did not last for long: soon the essential justice of the struggle would rally him, and he would plunge into the organization of a new operation.

The setbacks drew Britain and Free France closer together. At this period there was real accord between Churchill and his Cabinet and de Gaulle. Though the fact that they were so alike in character in many ways prevented the two autocrats at the head of affairs from ever becoming really close friends, Churchill and de Gaulle gained such admiration for each other's qualities in those difficult days that they have remained friends ever since. And with Eden the French leader developed a firm and lasting friendship, as he did with many of the other war leaders, including Attlee, Alexander, the First Lord of the Admiralty, Ernest Bevin, Herbert Morrison, and R. A. Butler.

But at this time de Gaulle had the hardest task of all the war leaders. Still conscious of the weakness of his organization, of the currents of opposition which flowed even in his inner councils, of the fact that even now some in the British Government felt that the Vichy regime might be used to the advantage of the Allies, he had to battle on alone. He has paid ungrudging tribute, in which there is no suggestion of sarcasm, to the way in which his British colleagues, at the same time that they gave him their friendship, also turned on him the full power of their political and diplomatic machine, using every device to bring him to their way of thinking. "What concentration of effort, what variety of procedure, what insistence, by turns gracious, pressing, or menacing, the English are capable of employing in order to obtain satisfaction!" he wrote later in his memoirs.

15

Triumph of Saint-Pierre and Miquelon

❧ De Gaulle was in Brazzaville in May 1941, when the British Government decided to move into Syria and the Lebanon to liquidate the threat of German air concentrations on Syrian airfields which an agreement between Pétain and Hitler made imminent. German bombers in Syria would have seriously threatened the British effort in Palestine.

De Gaulle had for long been of the opinion, in which he was opposed by Muselier and some others of his own supporters, that the end of the war would mark the end of the French mandate in the Levant. In the same way as he was, in 1958, to offer independence to the French Empire overseas without conditions, he now proposed to offer it to Syria and the Lebanon. Churchill agreed, and insisted that the communiqué should be in the joint name of Britain and France. De Gaulle resisted this on the grounds that Syria and the Lebanon were the responsibility of France alone.

The British Government had issued on May 15 a statement in the House of Commons that because the Vichy Government had agreed, contrary to the conditions of the armistice agreement between France and Germany, that German planes might use Syrian airports, the British Government had decided to bomb these airports. At the same time it was made known to de Gaulle—who had

flown to Cairo—that the question as to whether his Free
French troops should take any part in the land operations
against Syria and the Lebanon would be left entirely to the
General commanding the French troops in Palestine. It
would not be possible for the British further to reinforce
the French, because all available reserves were required
for operations in Iraq.

De Gaulle has since been attacked for allowing the Free
French Forces to take part in the campaign in Syria.
Muselier claims that he had warned the General that such
an action would have a disastrous effect on French public
opinion. He has claimed also that General Leclerc was of
the same opinion.

De Gaulle knew, however, to what extent the British
were stretched at that time in the Middle East. In the
Libyan Desert the Ninth Australian Division under General Sir Leslie Morshead, with British support, was surrounded in Tobruk, and a thin line of defense held Rommel
back from Egypt at Hellfire Pass. In Iraq the first rumblings
of the Rashid Ali revolt made it essential for a watch to
be kept there. Only the Seventh Australian Division, not
fully equipped or trained, was available for the Syrian
campaign. No tanks were available, and little in the way
of truck transport. The First Cavalry Division was the
mobile spearhead of the advance, and there was on one
occasion the absurd situation of cavalry attacking French
light tanks with cavalry swords, no doubt heroic, but
suicidal, and certainly indicative of the lack of modern
arms available to the Allies.

De Gaulle, in view of his previous stand that any question of the declaration of the independence of Syria and
the Lebanon should come from France and not from
Britain, had no alternative but to agree to send his own

small and ill-equipped force into Syria with the object of capturing Damascus. The prophets of woe, and Muselier led these, had no other suggestion to offer, and their opposition has since been proved amply wrong.

The Vichy French fought with great tenacity, mainly because of the attitude of some of their colonial units, but also, as de Gaulle himself said in a cable to Churchill, "in great part on account of honor, a taste for the work, and because of the ingrained discipline on the part of the officers, who, having been given an order, carried it out."

By June 18, anniversary of the foundation of Free France, the Vichy French forces under General Dentz were on the point of capitulation. M. Couty, the political director of the French High Commissioner in the Levant, asked the American Consul-General in Beirut what conditions the British and Free French (Gaullists was the word he used) required for an end of hostilities. De Gaulle stated categorically that the only bases for an armistice were that all troops and civil servants should be guaranteed honorable treatment; that the rights of France in the Levant should be maintained; that France should be represented in the Levant by supporters of the Free French. He demanded that all troops and civil servants who wished to remain in the Levant should be allowed to do so with their families, the rest being repatriated to France later, and he stressed that care should be taken to see that their choice was freely made.

The conditions relayed by the British authorities to General Dentz were very different from these. The agreement of Saint-Jean-d'Acre was between Britain and Vichy, and it handed over Syria and the Lebanon to British control without a mention of France. There was no attempt by the Vichy French to safeguard French interests, and their only concern was to prevent the Free French from meeting the troops and civil servants in order to invite them to join de Gaulle.

Muselier in London attempted to mobilize opinion in the French Empire Defense Council against the agreement by alleging that de Gaulle had concurred in an armistice without consulting his colleagues in any way; that de Gaulle had promised independence to the Lebanon and to Syria without securing any advantages for France.

De Gaulle's reaction to the armistice was to seek an immediate meeting in Cairo with Oliver Lyttelton (now Lord Chandos), the British Minister of State. "The armistice proposals are totally unacceptable," de Gaulle said. "They would mean that authority in the Levant would pass from France to Britain. It is Free France, and Free France alone, which has the right to exercise that authority in the name of France. Also it is imperative that I should have the opportunity of rallying as many as possible of the troops of General Dentz to the side of Free France. Therefore not only can I not agree to be kept away from a source of recruits, but I also cannot agree that our common effort in the Levant should only be to install Britain in authority there."

Lyttelton drew attention to the fact that it was a common cause in which they were fighting, and that in the accord of August 7, 1940, de Gaulle had agreed to recognize the authority of the British command.

"I have faithfully carried out that agreement," de Gaulle reminded him. "But that referred only to strategy and the fight against the common enemy. The agreement did not cover the sovereignty, the political beliefs, or the territories of France. When one day we land on the soil of Metropolitan France again, will you argue that the accord of August

7, 1940, gives you the right to govern France? I insist on being allowed to contact those who have been under Vichy. That is to your advantage also."

"But the armistice is already signed," Lyttelton reminded him.

"It does not bind Free France. I refuse to ratify it."

"What are you going to do, then?"

"I shall withdraw the forces of Free France from the command of the British G.O.C. After July 24—that is, in three days' time—I shall order our troops to contact those of General Dentz and to take over all matériel that is French. You know what I and all who follow me have done and will do for our alliance. We should regret very much any alteration in this situation. But if this alliance should operate to the detriment of France we would prefer to suspend our engagements so far as Britain is concerned. In that case we should pursue the war against the enemy by the best means in our power."

De Gaulle also cabled Churchill to confirm that the Free French considered the convention of Saint-Jean-d'Acre as opposed in its very foundations to the military and political interests of Free France—that is to say, of France—and also exceedingly damaging to her dignity. "I hope that you feel that such an attitude on the part of the British in a matter so vital to us will aggravate our difficulties considerably, and will have what I regard as deplorable consequences on the task we have undertaken."

This blunt speaking alarmed the members of the Empire Defense Council in London. Muselier, Cassin, and Captain d'Argenlieu, of the Free French Navy, cabled de Gaulle at once to protest at the risk being taken with the Franco-British alliance. On that alliance alone could they hope for the restoration of France and her Empire, they said.

Though, indeed, there was alarm and much annoyance in British Government circles in London at the course events had taken, these feelings were not, as the members of the Free French Defense Council assumed, directed entirely at de Gaulle. With the German advance into Russia and the difficult situation of the British forces in Tobruk and the Western Desert, Syria and the Lebanon were very much a secondary consideration of Churchill's. More than at any other period of the war the local commanders were allowed to handle the situation on their own initiative, and there was considerable confusion, not only in the relations with the Free French, but also in the organization of the British forces in the area. There were at that time thoughts on the matter of British troops entering Turkey—at the invitation of the Turkish Government —and this move was constantly in the foreground of the planning, and as constantly pushed into the background by the continued hesitation of the Turks. In the Levant at that time military organization was chaotic.

Lyttelton, in consultation with London, was able to assure de Gaulle that there was no thought of any action which would prejudice the Franco-British alliance. Almost at once, when the atmosphere had become cordial again, General Wilson, the British Commandant in the Levant, decided to proclaim martial law in the area, and this brought a French assurance that if he did that they would ignore it and would consider that the alliance was broken.

De Gaulle instructed Cassin to see Eden and to tell him that the interference of the British authorities in the Levant would gain them advantages which would be small compared with the disadvantages that would follow a quarrel between Free Frence and Britain. "Rather than continue like this," de Gaulle told Eden, "we would go our own way and let you go yours."

Lyttelton immediately assured de Gaulle that the troubles had come through faults in communication, and perhaps of comprehension. That, no doubt, was true, for at the time there was the utmost confusion in the military thinking in the Levant. This resulted in wholesale breaking of the armistice agreements by the Vichy French, the loss of several thousands of fighting men who might well have come over to the Free French, but instead were allowed to be returned to the supervision of Germany, and a black market in money and goods between the Levant and Palestine which was as vicious as anything seen in any theater of war.

De Gaulle, through his second-in-command, General Catroux, was in a position to have brought Syria and the Lebanon fully into the war on the side of the Allies. Catroux particularly understood the people of the two countries and was trusted by them. Syria and the Lebanon were French in every way—in language, in living conditions, and in thought. The British were as far from understanding their mentality as they were from understanding the mentality of the Jews in Palestine and the Palestine Arabs. Thus, while unnecessary meddling was going on in Syria and the Lebanon, intrigues and plots were building up in Palestine, which made the war of 1948 inevitable. Many who saw service in the Middle East in the war years were soon to realize the responsibility of those in command for the trouble in the area as soon as war was ended.

De Gaulle and Catroux saw this danger in 1941. They tried by all means in their power to prevent it. The visionary offer of independence to Syria and the Lebanon was an act of statesmanship which de Gaulle has since repeated with success in other parts of the French Empire. But, as in the case of the misguided British leaders on the spot—and Wilson, Sir Edward Spears, and Glubb Pasha cannot be absolved from the major blame—there was also a lack of comprehension in London in both British and French circles.

The Empire Defense Council in London saw only a de Gaulle who had lost control of his senses in his passionate attachment to the cause of France. They again cabled him admitting their fright that the whole alliance was coming apart. And they received in reply a message which was pure de Gaulle: "Our greatness and our strength consist only in our intransigence in what concerns the rights of France. We shall have need of that intransigence right to the banks of the Rhine," he declared.

But it was inevitable that he must return to London to face the Empire Defense Council. He took his time over the return, and did not set out before he had visited Damascus and Beirut and had been acclaimed by the crowds there. He reached London in September 1941.

Muselier had a trial of strength with de Gaulle. He found, however, that de Gaulle was supported by the British Government, and immediately there was an adjustment of views which resulted in the crisis passing. But to a great extent the energies of de Gaulle in prosecuting the war effort were being dissipated by the intrigues of his subordinates. He was all the time aware that indiscipline and scandal were nullifying the efforts of the Free French movement at a time when its power was growing. Muselier, who was himself filled with patriotic fervor, had made it plain, first that he wished to become the President of the French National Committee, then, when he saw that that would not be accepted, hurriedly changed his demand to the position of Vice-president of the Committee. Such maneuverings, even if they were for the good of France, did not make for smooth working.

De Gaulle, realizing that the struggle was won, was firm but cordial to his second-in-command, who accepted an ordinary place on the National Committee under protest. His fears he openly expressed to the British Admiralty. That, again, was not helpful.

For a long time past—as far back as September 1940, indeed—de Gaulle had been concerned about the islands of Saint-Pierre and Miquelon, tiny pieces of France lying to the south of Newfoundland and still under the jurisdiction of the Vichy Government. De Gaulle had many times drawn the attention of the British Government to the absurdity of a situation that two islands from which reconnaissance of vital Allied convoys could be carried out should continue to be left in the hands of the enemy. The hesitation on Churchill's part was almost entirely due to Canadian and United States attitude, which was not noticeably pro-de Gaulle—in fact, was in the main based on the idea that a great majority of Frenchmen were anti-Free France. This was Roosevelt's opinion, and one to which he clung with tenacity even after there had been many signs to the contrary.

News reached de Gaulle in November 1941 that in talks between them the United States and Canada had agreed that the radio transmitter on Saint-Pierre was to be taken over by Canada. No word of this was given to the Free French, which was bad enough in de Gaulle's eyes, but also his intelligence informed him that there were some in Canada who felt that Saint-Pierre and Miquelon, once in Canadian hands, should be forever part of Canada.

De Gaulle and his National Committee hurriedly made their plans to forestall the North American allies. The Japanese attack on Pearl Harbor on December 7 aided them, for it drove out of American minds, at least for the time, the plan to take over the unimportant islands near

Newfoundland. But de Gaulle had no such distraction. Muselier was sent on a visit to Canada to inspect the submarine "Surcouf" in Halifax Harbor.

On December 13 the United States seized fourteen French ships in American harbors, including the giant Atlantic liner "Normandie," and this action more than ever convinced de Gaulle that he must act at Saint-Pierre. On the same day Muselier informed him, "The United States is about to take over the West Indies [Saint-Pierre and Miquelon were administered from Martinique], and I believe that it is imperative to safeguard the sovereignty of France, which Free France will represent in our forthcoming operations."

De Gaulle approached Churchill, who was sympathetic and also promised to take the matter up with Canada and the United States, though he felt that the islands were more their concern than his own. De Gaulle therefore cabled Muselier to inform him that there could be no question of an answer being received before the date on which they had planned to take over the islands and thus the Admiral should go ahead.

On December 18 the United States Government informed Eden that the United States was entirely opposed to any suggestion of the Free French landing on Saint-Pierre and Miquelon. The same day de Gaulle, still using his secret means of transmission, which was never once discovered by the other Allies, cabled Muselier: "The solution is for you to take action in Saint-Pierre on your own initiative. I repeat that I shall cover you entirely on this subject."

In his order to proceed, de Gaulle also said: "We know for certain that the Canadians intend to destroy the radio-telephone installation on Saint-Pierre, and I therefore order you to carry out the rallying of Saint-Pierre and Miquelon by your own means and without saying anything to the foreigners. I take the entire responsibility for this operation, which has become indispensable to conserve France's overseas possessions."

Muselier had to cable de Gaulle that he would proceed as soon as possible, but that the snowstorms then affecting eastern Canada had frozen the guns and torpedo tubes of his ships. But he received a further message from the Committee in London that they had word that the Americans had ascertained that the French Admiral Georges Robert, the Commander-in-Chief in Martinique, was sending two cruisers to Saint-Pierre. Muselier set sail with three frigates, the "Mimosa," the "Alysse," and the "Aconite," and the submarine "Surcouf" on December 23, and landed on Saint-Pierre on Christmas Eve.

Churchill was in Washington at the time, and was able to see at firsthand the reactions of the American Government to the news. The British Government had all along known that action was to be taken, and they had at no time made any attempt to hamper de Gaulle's preparations. Muselier had been taken to Canada at the time required; he had been allowed to retain command of his ships and to take them out on exercises when it was apparent that he intended to carry out the rallying of the islands. The repeated parleying of de Gaulle with Eden and his messages to Churchill revealed that they not only knew of his intentions, but approved of them. Churchill in his speeches and conversations in Canada also made it quite plain that he supported de Gaulle's action.

But America reacted as if the Free French had seized the District of Columbia. Cordell Hull had conceived a deep-seated hatred of de Gaulle, and he did his utmost

to see that Roosevelt should condemn de Gaulle's action.
The American administration attempted to suggest that
this was an act of piracy, the antithesis of democratic
action; that the people of Saint-Pierre and Miquelon were
not on the side of Free France. But the people of the
United States gave the news a great reception, for at last
someone had reversed the dismal trends of the past few
months; someone had had the courage to take action to
deny the Axis the use of a radio station that was helping
to send British—and North American—ships to the bottom. The fact that not a shot had to be fired and that the
people came out to welcome Muselier and his Free French
sailors was not lost on the American people, but it was
on Hull. And when the islands voted in their referendum
and gave de Gaulle 98 per cent of the votes Hull seemed
even more annoyed at being proved wrong, and still refused to accept the facts. He issued a statement which
ran: "Our preliminary reports show that the action taken
by the so-called Free French ships at Saint-Pierre-
Miquelon was an arbitrary action contrary to the agreement of all parties concerned, and certainly without the
prior knowledge or consent in any sense of the United
States Government. This Government has inquired of the
Canadian Government as to the steps that Government is
prepared to take to restore the *status quo* of these islands."
The answer to the last sentence from the Canadian
Government was, in effect, "Nothing."

The use of the term "so-called Free French" greatly
offended de Gaulle. It offended many others besides—
Churchill and other members of the British Government
and millions of Americans. It has been said that de Gaulle's
action in taking Saint-Pierre-Miquelon back into the hands
of France was one of the great blunders of the war. In

fact, the attitude taken by the American administration following that trivial action was a major blunder. By making a point of keeping de Gaulle and his Free French administration out of consultations—even by excluding them from the United Nations Declaration, despite the fact that both Eden and Lord Halifax interceded on their behalf—the American Government hampered many actions in the future in which Free French participation would have been invaluable.

But the most far-fetched complaint made by Hull in regard to the Saint-Pierre episode was that because de Gaulle had taken matters into his own hands Germany had decided to send more troops to North Africa. It must have been known to the United States administration, as it was to Britain and Free France, that Germany had been preparing for action in Africa even before the first days of the Free French movement—from the time of the abortive attack on Dakar.

This attitude towards de Gaulle also prevented the rapid freeing of the other territories of France still under Vichy —Martinique, French Guiana, La Réunion, Madagascar. It paid no attention either to the strategically placed French possessions in the Pacific, which were all pro-Free France and which were of vital importance to the American and Allied effort in the war against Japan.

The attitude of America in respect of Saint-Pierre and Miquelon—and at the outset Roosevelt had been constrained to regard it merely as an incident of little importance—in fact directed the American President's views into channels which remained for long adverse to de Gaulle.

16

"Too Proud to Bow My Head"

❧ There was another important repercussion of the Saint-Pierre and Miquelon incident. Muselier, on his return to Britain, had not made any secret of the fact that he had not agreed with the methods by which it had been carried out, even to the extent of saying that it was not democratic. This complex character, whose patriotism and skill as a naval commander were undoubted, was now offering de Gaulle the command of the French forces that would liberate Madagascar.

At that very moment the plans for a British assault on the French island in the Indian Ocean had been completed, and the first moves towards assembling the ships and men who would be engaged were being taken. De Gaulle was not told anything of this maneuver, and he himself went on with his own preparations, as he had from time to time during the preceding eighteen months.

At that time the stories circulating about the Free French were numerous and damaging. One told of a woman member of de Gaulle's cipher department who, returning at the urgent request of her chief, though ill with influenza, shivered so much in her office in the cold weather of winter that she broke the rules and switched on her electric fire (shut off for economy purposes). "How dare you switch on your fire?" demanded her superior. "I have influenza

and should be in bed," the woman replied. "In any case,
I notice that the General has his fire on." "That is beside
the point," acidly rejoined the man. "He offered to switch
it off."

Another story told of the General was: "He never sends
back the elevator for the next man."

"There must be something wrong with him—he asked
me how I was," was another favorite joke.

Indeed, despite the accusations of Muselier and the rest
of the malcontents, de Gualle did make very few mistakes.
If he was often so much in the clouds that he could not
adequately control those who worked, and often schemed,
beneath him it was only because all the time his thoughts
were on France—his *marotte* (obsession), as his French
subordinates called it. His closest associates—Gaston
Palewski (called "Eminence Grise" by the junior members
of the office staff), Coulet and Serreulles, his aides, Moret,
Pleven, and Boris were all the time immovably loyal.
Serreulles was in every way the most popular member of
the headquarters staff, and most who came to see the
General have paid tribute to the unfailing charm and
kindness they received from Serreulles—attentions which
did much to soften any animosity the callers sometimes
had towards de Gaulle.

But there was no consoling Muselier. It became obvious
to de Gaulle that his brilliant but turbulent naval officer
could not continue to act as he was doing inside the
headquarters staff of the Free French—that, in fact, there
were two separate movements inside Free France. Moreover, he realized that Muselier had maintained for a long
time his own secret communication systems, and, when
at last the code was broken, de Gaulle was able to realize
the extent to which his own actions had been called into

question by his second-in-command. He taxed Muselier
with this at a meeting in Carlton Gardens on March 2,
1942. Muselier's answer was that de Gaulle could have
known of this only by "buying" one of his (Muselier's)
officers.

At a stormy meeting of the National Committee on
March 3 Muselier resigned from it. De Gaulle insisted that
this resignation must be made in writing, and Muselier, in
a letter the same day, confirmed his resignation from the
National Committee, but said that he was ready to take
part in any military operation which de Gaulle judged to
be good and which was in agreement with the policy of
their Allies.

Muselier was openly of the opinion now that de Gaulle
was "an apprentice-dictator, so much more dangerous for
France as he accumulated faults and revealed himself
more incompetent."

Muselier tried one more stand against de Gaulle. However, when it became apparent that the British Government had no intention of supporting Muselier, he accused
them of encouraging de Gaulle in his dictatorial acts, not
for one moment accepting the fact that de Gaulle had
never deviated in his actions towards Muselier from the
very first days of the Free French movement in June 1940.
De Gaulle had then made it clear that he was in command
and intended Muselier to obey him. From that day de
Gaulle never altered his attitude towards the Admiral, but
Muselier himself had many times changed his course,
which was as wayward as the winds of the seas that he
knew so well.

De Gaulle had other worries besides Muselier. On May
5, 1942, he was astonished to be told by a news agency
that British forces had landed at Diego Suarez, in Mada-

gascar. The General was as staggered by this blow as by anything that had happened to him from the very start of the war. But, instead of meeting Eden immediately, as the British Foreign Secretary had asked, de Gaulle decided to remain incommunicado while he thought over every aspect of the situation. "I must remember that this is again only one incident in our long struggle for France," he told his closest advisers in Carlton Gardens.

When it became evident that Darlan had sent a message to the Governor of Madagascar which ran, "Do not forget that the British betrayed us in Flanders; they treacherously attacked us at Mars-el-Kebir, at Dakar, and in Syria, and by bombing they have assassinated civilians in our home territory," de Gaulle realized that perhaps it was for the best that no men of Fighting France, which his movement now called itself, had been engaged in this battle against Frenchmen.

When at last he saw Eden, de Gaulle demanded that with an end of the fighting Madagascar should be handed over to the jurisdiction of "France Combattante." After some equivocation Eden agreed that the British Government would publish an official statement that Madagascar would be administered by the National Committee of Fighting France, and would through that committee cooperate with the United Nations.

It was a great triumph for de Gaulle. In a radio talk to France he reiterated that he would never allow the division of France and her Empire, nor their neutralization. But his triumph was to be short-lived. The stubborn resistance of the Vichy forces on Madagascar meant that all the old sores were reopened, and Vichy had new ammunition to try to persuade the French people of the iniquity of Fighting France and de Gaulle.

One bright light shone out on his horizon at that time. At Bir Hakeim, in the Libyan Desert, General Koenig and his Fighting French were assigned a "box" to hold against Rommel's Afrika Corps. Three divisions of German and Italian troops attacked the "box," in which Koenig's First Division was entrenched. In the first attack of May 26-27, 1942, out of eighty Italian tanks thirty-five were destroyed by Koenig's men. Day after day the attacks were repulsed, with heavy casualties on both sides. But still Bir Hakeim held out. In the end, after sixteen days and nights of almost incessant attack, the remains of the garrison fought their way out.

De Gaulle cabled Koenig: "General Koenig, know and tell your men that France looks towards you and is proud of you."

It now became obvious to de Gaulle that matters of the greatest importance were happening in Africa. The Fighting French intelligence was sending reports to London which revealed that preparations were going on suggesting a landing in Africa of some size. Throughout Africa there was a slackening in the size and frequency of merchant convoys—always a sure sign that something was afoot.

De Gaulle sensed also a certain uneasiness on the part of the British Government leaders with whom he came into contact. Both Churchill and Eden went out of their way to assure him that the Allies had no designs on French territory overseas. De Gaulle told them that he was disturbed at the continued opposition of Roosevelt to both the Fighting French and to himself. Churchill soothed de Gaulle by reminding him that he, Churchill, was also disposed to yield to American persuasion, and then to raise himself again to his old stature.

To this de Gaulle replied with one of his most famous rejoinders. "You can do that," he said, "because you rest on the basis of a solid State, a mobilized nation, a united Empire, and possess great armies. But where are my means? Yet I have charge of the interests and the destinies of France. It is too heavy a burden, but I am too proud to bow my head."

De Gaulle realized the extent to which Britain had to take second place to the United States in the matter of planning and direction. Not for one moment did he ever doubt the goodwill of Churchill, but also not for one moment did he think that he was being treated as an equal by the British Prime Minister. The incident of Saint-Pierre and Miquelon had convinced him that he must keep his own counsel in all that affected France, while still doing everything to help and nothing to hamper the united war effort. When he learned that all the secrecy and the deception were concerned with an Allied landing in North Africa he said nothing. He made no complaint that he had not been informed, for he also knew that Roosevelt had demanded that the landing should be completely an American affair, except for British ships, without which the operation could never be carried out. When British troops were added to the project it was first decided to dress them in American uniforms.

Roosevelt's intelligence reports were almost completely wrong. He was sure that de Gaulle and his Fighting French were unpopular in North Africa. Roosevelt was convinced, indeed, that this was the case in France itself. Yet by the time the Allied landings came in North Africa most members of the French Resistance looked on de Gaulle as France herself. He alone represented to them the hopes of the future, a ray of light in the darkness.

When de Gaulle urged Churchill to land in France and to leave North Africa to fall into his hands without a struggle he was not advocating a wild scheme. At that time there would in all probability have been more French support for the Allied cause than came later, after the bitterness of the North Africa invasion and the renewed suspicions of Allied motives.

But Roosevelt had written to Churchill: "In my view it is essential that de Gaulle be kept out of the picture and be permitted to have no information whatever, regardless of how irritated and irritating he may become." This was a phrase that might have been calculated to drive de Gaulle to extremes, but the long months of waiting and hoping had given him a control of his feelings that was even greater than it had been in the past. All this knowledge of the attitude of his Allies only made the lonely Frenchman more determined than ever to keep his eyes firmly fixed on his target—the rebirth of France. That was all that mattered to him then.

In all these trying days his wife, little though she entered into his official life, was by his side as much as possible, listening to his difficulties and helping at times with advice. They had a house at Berkhamsted, and they had had a cottage in Shropshire. But these knew the General only at weekends, when he walked mile after mile with Yvonne by his side, and for a few hours managed to take himself away from the worries of London.

It was on Sunday, November 8, 1942, that de Gaulle heard the news of the Allied landings in Casablanca, Algiers, and Oran. He learned that there was heavy fighting, and that Pétain had answered Roosevelt's appeal for moderation and understanding by stating, "We are attacked; we shall defend ourselves; this is the order I am giving."

De Gaulle masked his anger and his anguish. He did his utmost by radio appeals to the troops and the colonists in North Africa to bring the fighting to an end. He cooperated loyally with the American and British Governments in the days that followed.

But when, in desperation over the continued resistance of the French in North Africa, the American Government came to an agreement with Darlan, the French High Commissioner, de Gaulle rebelled at once. Eisenhower, who had commanded the Allied landings, had declared to Roosevelt that only Darlan could take over the position of Pétain—the Germans had by then occupied all France —and in this Eisenhower was supported by Giraud, who had escaped from France and reached Algiers by way of Gibraltar. Giraud, in fact, had been Eisenhower's first choice for the leadership of French North Africa.

De Gaulle's rage was devastating, and for once he did not attempt to contain it. In his own hand he penned a letter to Roosevelt and delivered it to Admiral Stark, Chief of the American Naval Staff in London, through Commander Kittredge, the American liaison officer. "Mr. President," the letter ran, "you may buy treachery from traitors, but you will not pay for it with the honor of France. C. de Gaulle."

The letter was never dispatched. It is perhaps as well. Stark kept it back until the following morning, by which time de Gaulle had calmed to the extent of asking that it should not be sent. Instead the General issued a statement to the effect that there was not the least possibility of Fighting France accepting Darlan as High Commissioner in North Africa. He would not budge from that fundamental stand.

De Gaulle also issued a statement over the radio that he and the National Committee would assume no responsibility for what was taking place in North Africa, and if the negotiations in train meant the conservation of the Vichy regime in North Africa they also would not be accepted by Fighting France. But a little later the B.B.C. refused permission for de Gaulle to broadcast a declaration from the whole of the French Resistance. "General de Gaulle is unquestionably the chief of the Resistance, and more than ever carries all the country behind him," it ran. "In no case will we admit that the rallying of those responsible for military and political treachery to the Allied cause shall now be considered redress for the crimes they have committed. We demand that the destinies of North Africa shall be put back into the hands of General de Gaulle."

The American Government had informed Eisenhower that the United States did not trust Darlan, but they had made it just as plain that they did not trust de Gaulle any the more. The days which followed, though, in fact, tragic for the cause of the Allies and for France, had their measure of comedy. Roosevelt in particular committed the most elementary mistakes in handling the situation in North Africa, and Churchill made no outward effort to correct him.

De Gaulle at that time was in his most intransigent mood. The flood of intelligence reports which were reaching him from both France and North Africa convinced him that he had only to hold to his point of view to win the day. The brothers Emmanuel and Henri d'Astier de la Vigerie, both intimately connected with the Resistance, were invaluable to de Gaulle at that moment. General d'Astier, in December 1942, opened the first negotiations with Giraud. But it is astonishing that the British and American Governments, if they had the same information that was so readily available to de Gaulle, should have continued to sponsor Darlan and Giraud as preferable to him.

The summons to de Gaulle to attend the Casablanca Conference in 1942, of which he had had no official warning, but of which he had, as usual, plenty of information, was brusque to the point of rudeness. Unless he came as ordered it would mean the complete withdrawal of Anglo-American support. Despite the personal insult, de Gaulle once again revealed that he was always prepared to put country before self. He swallowed his pride and decided to go to Casablanca, where the Chiefs of Staff still argued over the question of whether the Allied thrust into Europe should be through Italy or northern France. De Gaulle himself had all along been of the opinion that a thrust into northern France would prove the least costly venture, but at Casablanca only the American General Marshall had this view.

By continued attention to false premises the Roosevelt administration allowed themselves to lose sight of the great importance of the de Gaulle name in the common fight against Germany. France was the key to the struggle with Hitler, and France, represented by all the freedom fighters who planned to take over the key points once the liberating armies had landed, recognized and trusted only de Gaulle—not Churchill, nor Roosevelt, nor any of the Allied Generals, but only the disembodied voice which spoke to them over the radio and gave them hope which was usually borne out by events.

Roosevelt and Churchill, by even considering cooperation with Darlan, whom the French Resistance regarded as a traitor, and with Giraud, whom they felt had done nothing for France, alienated the Resistance and put a brake on much of their activities.

That de Gaulle should have been met in Algeria, a prov-

ince of France, with armed secret agents who watched
his every movement, though, in fact, they also were being
watched by the agents of de Gaulle, and that he was
forced to live within a barbed-wire encampment was to
him an affront to the dignity of France. He showed cold-
ness and austerity during the meetings. Roosevelt put this
down to his being a "prima donna," when in fact he was
merely registering his protest that France should be
treated as anything but an equal of the other Allies.

But Roosevelt was to commit his greatest blunder in re-
lation to the French leader by not recognizing the driving
force behind the man. The American President did not
realize the extent to which history had fashioned the character and the life of de Gaulle. To him it was matter for
humor that de Gaulle should link himself with the great
names of France's past. Roosevelt was not, in fact, prepared to listen to him, and merely used the General's
thesis of the importance to France in 1942 of the names
and achievements of her citizens in the past as the basis
of the joke about Charles de Gaulle believing himself to
be Joan of Arc.

Despite all the threats, all the entreaties of Britain and
America to give way over Giraud, de Gaulle remained
obdurate. The tide was eventually turned on May 15, after
there had been innumerable evidences that all French
North Africa was behind de Gaulle, by an announcement
from the National Council for the Resistance, meeting in
Paris under Jean Moulin, who had been parachuted into
France in a plane from Britain:

> All the movements, all the parties, of the Resistance of the
> North and South Zones, have on the eve of the departure of
> General de Gaulle for Algiers renewed to him, and thus to the
> National Committee, the assurance of their total devotion to the

principles which they embody, and of which they would not abandon a jot.

All the movements, all the parties, declare formally that the meeting foreshadowed [between de Gaulle and Giraud] should take place at the residence of the Governor-General of Algeria and between Frenchmen.

They affirm furthermore that the political problems cannot be excluded from the conversations; that the people of France will never admit the subordination of General de Gaulle to General Giraud, but demand the rapid installation in Algiers of a provisional Government under the presidency of General de Gaulle, General Giraud to be the Commander-in-Chief of the armed forces; that General de Gaulle shall remain the only leader of the French Resistance whatever the result of the negotiations.

Giraud appeared to give way, America appeared to give way, Britain appeared to give way. De Gaulle, in his moment of triumph, cabled Giraud to say: "It pleases me to work with you in the service of France." And to Eden, who congratulated him, yet added, "Do you know you cause us more trouble than all our European allies?" de Gaulle replied, "Of course; France is a Great Power."

It did not really matter that Roosevelt, having lost Darlan through assassination and Giraud by de Gaulle's intransigence, had provisionally installed Peyrouton, a former French Ambassador to the Argentine, as Governor-General in Algeria. But on the same day—May 30—that de Gaulle reached Algeria for his discussions with Giraud, Peyrouton wrote to the General, resigning his post and asking him to intercede with the military authorities so that he might be granted a post in the Army.

Giraud still was not done. With the almost unbelievable support of Eisenhower, he ordered the units of Fighting France out of French territory and into the neighborhood of Tripoli. In Algiers itself he appointed Muselier as Prefect of Police, with jurisdiction over an area around Algiers itself to a radius of almost forty miles. Muselier seized his opportunity with both hands. A report circulating in France itself at that time described Giraud's activities as being directed against de Gaulle and his friends by a group of men who had joined de Gaulle in 1940, but had quarrelled with him.

Giraud wrote to de Gaulle on June 2, and signed himself Commander-in-Chief, civil and military. He also ordered what was a virtual curfew in Algiers. De Gaulle calmly pointed out to Giraud that the atmosphere of a *Putsch* which his action created made a bad impression on observers. Giraud gave way.

The following day the seven members of the new Committee of National Liberation met—de Gaulle, Giraud, Catroux, Georges, Massigli, Monnet, and Philip. The Committee proclaimed that it was

> the central power of France; it would direct the French war effort everywhere and in all its forms; it would exercise the sovereignty of France; it would undertake the management and the defense of all French interests in the world; it would assume the authority in all the territories and over all the forces serving under the French National Committee or the Commander-in-Chief, civil and military. Until the Committee can restore its powers to the future provisional Government of the Republic it promises to restore all the French liberties, the laws of the Republic, the Republican regime, and to destroy entirely the arbitrary regime and the personal power imposed on the country to-day.

De Gaulle hurried to the radio on the following day and told all Frenchmen that their Government ruled now from Algiers while they waited the day of return to Paris.

And so throughout the summer and autumn of 1943 the National Committee worked in Algiers. Fighting France was not invited to take part in the landing in Sicily but was represented in the fighting in Italy. De Gaulle was not informed of the Italian pleas for an armistice on September 8. But Fighting France liberated Corsica in September and October.

On November 9 at a meeting of the National Committee de Gaulle was made President. There followed the first sitting of the Consultative Assembly, which had been formed on September 11. To this came Resistance fighters from France, and at this moving meeting the new France was planned.

17

Return to Paris

❧ De Gaulle took over the Villa des Glycines in Algiers, and there his wife joined him with their youngest daughter Anne, still suffering from ill-health and in need of constant nursing. Mme. de Gaulle slipped again into the background after a brief blaze of publicity—a journey to Gibraltar, where there was an official welcome by the Governor, and then a flight to Algiers in de Gaulle's personal aircraft.

At the Villa des Glycines she took on again the cloak of invisibility. If it had not been for the constant stream of knitted clothes for the babies of officers and men of the Fighting French which came from the villa one would have imagined she was not there. Her life—it would be considered drab by most people—was what she wanted. The General himself says, "By taste and by fitness our private life is very simple."

Not all the anxious questioning of the world's journalists or the eager eyes of the world's photographers have ever been able to show that the private life of the de Gaulles is any different from what it appears on the surface. Both Charles de Gaulle and his wife are as dedicated in their lives as are the members of a strict and closed monastic order.

For de Gaulle the stay in Algiers was one of the greatest activity. He realized that the Allies still neither trusted him nor wished to appear to be sponsoring his leadership of France.

His differences with Giraud had not been smoothed over by the apparent accord between them. But there was nothing of personalities in their rivalry, as had been the case with Muselier. Giraud looked at the whole problem of French rehabilitation from a different angle. He was a general of the old school. To him the men were soldiers who had to be cared for, guarded, trained, and disciplined. But they never became anything closer to him, as the ordinary soldier became to de Gaulle.

Giraud's attitude may be illustrated by two stories which are told of him. It is said that one day he was talking with a Deputy in Paris, who declared that he appeared to have no knowledge or interest in the workers. "Oh, yes, I have," Giraud replied. "As a small boy I used to take them oranges on Sundays, with my nurse."

While in North Africa soon after the Allied landings he visited the Superior of the White Fathers. "You are a Catholic and have taken an oath to Pétain," the Father reminded him, when they talked of the battle in progress. "My conscience is clear," Giraud replied. "There is an article of the Military Law which specifies that a soldier owes no obedience to a superior officer who has fallen into the hands of the enemy."

But, in fact, Giraud did not sever his connections with Pétain. Throughout his stay in Algeria he was in touch with the Marshal, believing that Pétain was really working for France against the Germans. Giraud's own secret agents were continually travelling back and forth to France, and often seriously prejudicing the lives and the actions of the official Resistance. It was, however, soon after the fusion of all the Resistance in the C.N.R. (Na-

tional Council for the Resistance), with Georges Bidault
as its President, that matters between de Gaulle and
Giraud came to a head. One of the most prominent Resistance leaders, Jacques Méderic, who had been to report to de Gaulle in Algiers, returned to France and
reached Paris safely, only to fall straight into the hands of
the police, making a routine check for black marketeers.
Méderic, when confronted by the Commissioner charged
with hounding down all the Gaullists of the city, declared
defiantly, "Now see how a Frenchman can die," and
dropped at the man's feet, killed by the cyanide pill which
all Resistance men carried.

Méderic's death was not the result of any action by
Giraud, but de Gaulle was only too well aware of the constant comings and goings of the Giraud agents, all supplied with cash and transport by the Americans. He knew
that there was a possibility that his friend could have been
betrayed by one of these. It was the affair Pucheu, however, which finally decided the Committee of the Liberation that Giraud must cease to be Commander-in-Chief,
civil and military.

Pierre Pucheu had been Laval's Minister of the Interior.
In 1942 he had escaped to Spain, and had then been al-
lowed by Giraud to come to Algiers, ostensibly to join the
Fighting French Army. Giraud made it a condition that
Pucheu came in secret, but he did anything but this, and
was soon showing himself openly.

Giraud put him under house arrest, but the Committee
of the Liberation insisted that Pucheu should be put on
trial. Pucheu was proved to have connived with the Germans in the execution of French workers, and was sentenced to death. Giraud gave evidence at the trial, but
spoke with great reticence about Pucheu. He also pleaded

with de Gaulle to postpone the execution. De Gaulle refused this request, and Pucheu was executed by a firing squad, himself defiantly giving the order "Fire."

The mud of the Pucheu affair stuck to Giraud, and finally the Committee of Liberation decided in April 1944 that he should cease to be Commander-in-Chief, but should be instead Inspector-General of the Armed Forces. Giraud refused, and retired to Mazagan. "I want to be Commander-in-Chief or nothing," he said.

There could now have been little doubt in the minds of the Allied war leaders that de Gaulle was not only the natural leader of all Frenchmen, but also the leader that all Frenchmen desired to have. But when, in early June, de Gaulle was urgently asked to come back to Britain, and was there told by Churchill that the landing in France was about to take place, there was still a disposition in the minds of the Americans, and to a less extent in the minds of the British, that de Gaulle was not the man to lead the French to final victory.

All this animosity towards the Frenchman who had rallied his country stemmed from the United States, and particularly from Roosevelt. The President never trusted de Gaulle, and after Roosevelt's visit to Morocco had given him the firm idea that he was to be the emancipator of the Arab peoples—he promised freedom to the Sultan of Morocco once the war was ended—he was convinced that de Gaulle was a dictator who would do everything to hinder any move towards freeing North Africa. Roosevelt was perhaps right in thinking that de Gaulle would not help to free North Africa: de Gaulle did not approach the problem of the North African territories from the point of view of colonies so much as of free associates of the French Empire.

Difficulties had persisted. Towards the end of April the British Government had made matters worse by declining to handle any more messages in code between de Gaulle in Algiers and his diplomatic and military delegations in London. De Gaulle reacted in his usual forthright way. He forbade his Ambassador in London, M. Viénot, and Koenig, his military liaison with Eisenhower, to have any further contact with the British authorities.

His own messages continued to travel by his own secret channels backward and forward between Algiers and London without hindrance. But the effect of this cutting off of cooperation between the French and the British, and therefore with the Allies, was most harmful.

At a time when the liaison between the Allies and the French Resistance should have been at its height a large degree of contact was lost. Whereas de Gaulle could have integrated the efforts of the Resistance more closely with that of the Allied armies when they landed, in fact there was still a good deal of heroic but misplaced action on the part of the French. The Resistance should have been an integral part of the Allied armies from the first day of landing, and not one that was left to act largely on its own.

The record of damage done by the Resistance to the German war effort shows how valuable it could have been if fully directed by those who knew what the Allied aims were. After the landing of the British and American armies in Normandy the Resistance went into action. Trains were derailed and locomotives destroyed. Eighteen hundred locomotives were put out of action in the first two months, and more than six thousand trucks severely damaged. Telephone and telegraph lines were broken, and whole stretches of railway line torn up. And the stream of reports and messages which came out of occupied territory totalled more than a hundred a day.

But de Gaulle knew that this was only a small proportion of the effort that the Resistance was really capable of if the whole plan of campaign had been taken as part of the general offensive.

When de Gaulle was asked to return to London on May 23 for the invasion of France he replied that it would be useless for him to come unless his position was accepted by Roosevelt as well as by the British Government. Three days later the Committee of the Liberation restyled itself "The Provisional Government of France." Still there was no sign that the Allies would accept this title. But on June 2 de Gaulle flew to London in Churchill's personal aircraft, and there found that the British Government was still arguing the point of view regarding the rightful Government of France.

It was the same viewpoint that the British and American leaders had taken throughout the war years. They were still incapable of believing that the Provisional Government of France was as representative of France as any that could now be found. Without offering any alternative, they were merely trying to ensure that de Gaulle did not take power. Knowing that France could not hold elections, that the French would not now accept Vichy legislators as representative, Roosevelt and Churchill both refused to admit that there was no alternative to de Gaulle and his followers.

Immediately before the Allied forces set sail for France, Eisenhower showed de Gaulle the proclamation which he intended to make to the French people, and in which, in effect, he took over control of the country. De Gaulle, of course, insisted that it would not do, but he could not move Eisenhower. De Gaulle learned later that Eisenhower was to make his proclamation over the radio on the morning of June 6, and that he, de Gaulle, would follow the General and speak to the French people. De Gaulle again refused to cooperate on the grounds that this would suggest that he concurred with the statement. He demanded that he be allowed to speak in the evening of the same day. This demand was granted, and de Gaulle made a memorable appeal to the people of France to take up the final struggle and gain the victory.

If de Gaulle had shown in those early days of June any weakness of will there would have been even greater difficulties for the Allied Powers in France than they eventually experienced. The obstinacy of the British and American Governments in the matter of de Gaulle approached the unbelievable, but there were noticeably some members of the British Government who did not agree with the line taken, among them Ernest Bevin.

De Gaulle's reception when, eight days after the first Allied landings in Normandy, he was allowed to return to France should again have shown Roosevelt and Churchill that for France at that time there was only one leader. Everywhere he went the General was met by vast crowds, who were by turns silenced by the depths of their emotion and almost hysterical in their delight and gratitude. Isigny, Grandcamp, and Bayeux were the places he visited after landing at Courseulles-sur-Mer, and from that time Bayeux came to be regarded by him as a place of pilgrimage to which he could return when France was at some crossroads of her history. He was to return there three years later, to make one of the most significant and far-reaching speeches of his life.

For a long time the question of de Gaulle's visiting America had been discussed. Always he had refused because the conditions were not acceptable to him or to Fighting France. But at last he agreed, and reached

Washington on July 6. There he found such cordiality that he was to be excused for thinking that at last Roosevelt's attitude towards him and the Fighting French had changed. In fact, he was to find that after all it was only the normal hospitality of the American people that he was enjoying, and that Roosevelt even now regarded him as a dangerous egotist who would not long survive the searching appraisal of the French people when the war was ended.

But de Gaulle was now concerned only with France again. He had the vision of French arms once more redeeming French soil. General Leclerc led his own division through Normandy with the other Allies; General de Lattre de Tassigny brought his troops northward from the Mediterranean. The gallant Resistance intensified their efforts, and hundreds died at the hands of the German troops. No fewer than twenty-eight of the ninety departments of France were captured by the Maquis, and with them almost 50,000 prisoners.

On August 25, 1944, de Gaulle once more entered Paris. He was filled with the emotion of the moment, so that for once even his impassive face had its flashes of indiscipline. The immense crowds which surged across the streets barring his progress like a great and turbulent tide were delirious in their excitement, and every moment more and more people poured out to greet him. The Germans were surrendering everywhere, and de Gaulle saw his own son with a German major who was arranging the surrender of the garrison of the city.

De Gaulle reached the Gare Montparnasse, and there received a report from General Leclerc on the situation in the city. Opposite them was the Brasserie Dumesnil, where de Gaulle had perhaps first set himself on the road

he was now taking. Now his mind for a moment seemed
far away, as he looked again at the well-remembered
scene, and soon he was making his way through the streets
towards the Ministry of War in the rue Saint-Dominique,
off the Boulevard Saint-Germain. At the top of Saint-
François-Xavier he was fired upon by a group of German
troops, still holding out in a building. De Gaulle and his
friends turned off into the rue Vaneau and rue Bourgogne,
both well-remembered streets of his prewar days at the
Ministry of Defense. They had not changed. The General
walked through the open gates of the Ministry of War,
into the courtyard, and the guard saluted him as if it was
only yesterday that he had last come through those gates
with Paul Reynaud.

In the building de Gaulle had the uncanny feeling that
all that had passed in the four years since he was last
there was only a dream. Nothing was out of place—no
desk, no table, no chair—even the papers on the desks
might have been there when he had left Paris in June
1940.

"Nothing was missing except the State," de Gaulle commented afterwards.

In the evening he walked with his aides, General Juin,
Le Troquer, Parodi, and de Luizet, to the Hôtel de Ville
to meet the people of Paris. His tall figure moved with
difficulty through the vast crowds, which pressed against
him, every man and woman trying just to touch his arm as
he passed. Almost every one was in tears.

At the Hôtel de Ville Georges Bidault, the President of
the Council for the Resistance, waited with André Tollet
and Marcel Floret, the Prefect, and welcomed de Gaulle.
The staircase was lined with Resistance fighters, presenting arms, tears in their eyes. De Gaulle himself described

"the sacred emotion" which filled them all and which exceeded anything they had experienced before.

In the office of the Prefect of the Seine Floret presented his officers. Then Bidault cried exultantly, "General, here before you are the National Council for the Resistance and the Parisian Liberation Committee. We ask you solemnly to proclaim the Republic before all the people assembled here to-day."

It was just the chance that de Gaulle required in this moment of public emotion. "The Republic has never ceased to exist," he reminded his listeners. "Free France, Fighting France, the French Committee for the Liberation, have represented the Republic one by one. Vichy was always null and void. I myself am the President of the Government of the Republic. Why, then, should I proclaim it?"

On the following day de Gaulle went on foot to the Arc de Triomphe. Was this the supreme moment of his life? He has given some suggestion that it was in his own writing. Paris had never seen a greater crowd in one small area than that which gathered to honor him. More than 2,000,000 people were in the streets, and for once there was a trace of pride in the way in which de Gaulle looked over that sea of eager faces and reached out as if to grasp all the millions of hands stretched out in gratitude towards him.

For a brief moment he gave way to the elation of the occasion, and responded as he has rarely done to any sentiment of the hour. But still as he walked through the crowds his mind was already turning away from the heady triumph of the liberation of Paris to the difficulties and the doubts of the future. Until he reached the Arc de Triomphe and saw before him the Champs-Elysées and

trod again the way of victorious France. Then nothing
could still the romantic de Gaulle. As he passed the statue
of Clemenceau he turned to salute, stiffly and smartly, the
effigy of the man who had inspired him through so many
years.

As the familiar landmarks came into his view his
thoughts were of their place in the story of France—Les
Tuileries, where France's emperors and kings once lived;
the Invalides (his mind marked off the names of the great
ones of France who lie below that massive dome—Napoleon, Turenne, Foch, Bertrand, and Grouchy); the
Louvre, where the Kings of France lived while they built
the country's greatness; the statues of Joan of Arc and of
Henri IV, the regenerator of France in the sixteenth and
seventeenth centuries; Notre-Dame; the Cité.

His mind ranged over all the history of France that was
etched in those ancient walls. He thought of St. Louis, of
Joan of Arc at the Porte Saint-Honoré, of Henri IV, of the
revolt of the Barricades, the massacre of St. Bartholomew,
the revolt against the King by the Fronde, the beheading
of the King and Queen on the Concorde, the destruction
of the ancient monarchy of France in the Tuileries, the
exile of Charles X and Louis-Philippe. And, as he marched
through the cheering crowds that were so crushed together on each side of the Champs-Elysées that they were
almost immovable, de Gaulle thought of the fact that too
many times in the course of two lifetimes invaders had
ridden in triumph down that very avenue. "If Paris this
evening shone with the greatness of France it also held
the lessons of bad days," said de Gaulle in his memoirs,
when describing the scene.

He had used the appeal of Bidault to make plain the
fact that he, Charles de Gaulle, was now the leader of

France herself, till such time as the people could say otherwise. Later that day at Notre-Dame he made plain that
no one who had collaborated with Vichy for any reason at
all could expect friendship or conciliation from him. The
Cardinal Archbishop of Paris, Monsignor Suhard, would
normally have greeted him at the door of the cathedral
when he came to the Mass in thanksgiving for the liberation of the city. But Suhard had received Pétain at the
cathedral only four months before, and he had officiated
at the funeral of Philippe Henriot. The C.N.R. felt that
this made it unthinkable that Mgr. Suhard should receive
the General, and de Gaulle did nothing to make them
change their minds.

As de Gaulle got down from his car there was a fusillade
of shots. It continued as he made his way into the cathedral and towards the choir. There were German snipers
inside in the high galleries who fired during the service.
There was no organ, because the electricity was off, and
as the singing began it was punctuated by the shots from
outside and inside. The choir sang the Magnificat, and de
Gaulle was transported back to his childhood, when he
had come to this place with his father and had been en-
chanted by the music. The wonderful singing of the hymn
thrilled him as even the experiences of the day had not
moved him. And perhaps for the first time the great cathedral rang to the cheers of the congregation when there
was a spontaneous shout of *"Vive de Gaulle!"* from all
those present. But within twenty minutes de Gaulle was
on his way back to the Ministry of War and at work on
the problems that faced the Allies.

On de Gaulle's mind was the problem of Pétain and of
those few who still openly gave allegiance to the old man.
Pétain had been taken into custody by the Germans, and

had thus not taken advantage of the offer made by de
Gaulle through his Commissioner, Henry Ingrand, at
Clermont-Ferrand, to place himself in the hands of the
Resistance in return for a promise of security. But Pétain's
fears in regard to the possibility of civil war, as expressed
in a note delivered to de Gaulle on August 25 by the
Marshal's envoy, Admiral Auphan, were groundless.
"Where is the civil war?" de Gaulle asked the Admiral.

There were no followers of Pétain in any of the departments of France after August 25, 1944. That was the
answer that de Gaulle gave to all his critics. All France
was his. Only he could say that by his exertions and his
will he had retained for France the honor of being able to
declare: "Beaten, we have been robbed of our provinces,
forced to pay reparations, but we have never lost our independence."

De Gaulle could be forgiven his moment of pride. But
it was short-lived. Sternly he schooled himself to forget
the triumphs so far won and to turn to the perils of the
future.

18

End of the Fourth Republic

❧ The Provisional Government of France came back to the homeland from Algiers on September 10, 1944, and on November 7 the Provisional Consultative Assembly met in the Senate building in Paris. M. Culotti, oldest member of the House of Deputies, was elected Speaker, and the 248 delegates were made up of 148 members of the Resistance in Metropolitan France, 28 members of the Resistance from overseas, 12 from the Empire, and 60 former deputies elected before 1939. These were chosen in direct proportion to the number of seats their parties had held before the war.

De Gaulle's position was one of great difficulty, for he had at his disposal mainly men who were prepared to give their allegiance to policies of the Left: no one would admit to having views to the extreme Right in case he were accused of being Fascist. Because of this equivocation de Gaulle could never be sure of the political reliability of every Deputy—any more than he could of the man's moral standards—and there were undoubtedly several active collaborators and black marketeers in the first Assembly.

In Algiers it had always been planned to bring back self-government to France through the municipal councils. But France was liberated as if by a tidal wave, and therefore the Central Government came into being before any

one local council. France was a devastation of broken telephone lines and destroyed roads and railways. It was not
possible to organize quickly local elections: there were no
electoral rolls and no machinery for assembling them
again.

De Gaulle recognized that he must show himself to
France without delay as the head of the Central Government. He at once set out on a whistle-stop tour, by air and
by rail and by road. What he saw he found disheartening.
Everywhere local dictators, who had taken charge immediately after liberation, were exercising their authority.
In one place he was met by the prefect of a town and a
crowd of officials and uniformed officers of field rank. De
Gaulle was pleasant enough with the man, but turned
quickly and inquired who the rest were. "My staff, sir,"
the prefect replied. "Mine," de Gaulle said, indicating his
aide, Captain Claude Guy.

He was equally short with his own Ministers when it
became too obvious that they were pursuing sectarian
lines of policy. In those first few months de Gaulle had
many times to rebuke his Ministers in the sharpest terms.
It is said that on one occasion, tiring of Ramadier's insistence on bringing forward food rationing in his role of
Minister of Food, de Gaulle snapped, "I did not bring
Fighting France into being to discuss dried beans."

He was learning politics the hard way, as he had had
to learn diplomacy. His troubles were not eased by the
fact that the other Allied leaders still insisted on regarding
themselves as on a different level from de Gaulle. In order
to see that France was accorded the same treatment as the
rest, de Gaulle went to Moscow on December 2, 1944,
and eight days later signed the twenty-year Franco-Soviet
Pact. What might have been a triumph, however, was

spoiled two months later when Stalin neglected to invite France to be present at the Yalta Conference. It left de Gaulle with the feeling that the Soviet Union could be trusted as little as could Britain and America.

The National Council for the Liberation had begun to have its disagreements with de Gaulle within a few days of the end of the liberation celebrations in Paris. De Gaulle and his Cabinet had decreed that in future the official police force should be responsible for public order. This meant that the civic guard would no longer exist. The C.N.R. and the Communist Party both fought the decision, and asked de Gaulle for his terms.

"The Government does not make terms: it makes laws, and it will see that those laws are obeyed," the General replied coldly to a delegation.

In reply the Communist Party issued a statement: "Once more the head of the Government has taken the responsibility of treating the French Resistance as a negligible quantity, an attitude which will be bitterly resented."

De Gaulle insisted that the F.F.I. (Forces Françaises de l'Intérieur) should be incorporated into the Army. This suggestion also met with the greatest opposition. But he realized that a great part of the F.F.I. was made up of Communists or of Frenchmen whose Left-wing ideas led them to think they were Communist. In these circumstances it was dangerous to leave arms in the hands of people who might not hesitate to use them against the established State.

De Gaulle was denounced by the Communist press once more as a Fascist, despite the fact that on September 13 at the Palais de Chaillot he had declared that the nation must control the main sources of public wealth. In swift order he requisitioned the Renault car works, sequestered the Paris Gas Company, nationalized the coal mines and the merchant marine. No country, other than a Communist State, has so quickly taken into public control so many differing enterprises as did de Gaulle's Government in the three months following the liberation.

But none of these actions did much to solve the country's problems. There were 2,000,000 Frenchmen in slavery in Germany. Everywhere, particularly in the north of the country, bridges had been destroyed and roads cut. Not one bridge remained on any road crossing the Seine, the Loire, the Rhône. Railway stations and yards, signal boxes, and railway repair shops had been destroyed over a great many of the railway systems: 115 stations were completely destroyed. Nearly 2,000 miles of railway line had been uprooted, and 1,900 rail bridges and 27 tunnels destroyed. Fewer than 3,000 of the 17,000 locomotives in use before the war still existed, and only half the 460,000 freight cars and 13,500 of the 36,000 passenger coaches. Half the fleet of trucks had been destroyed, and the majority of the country's canals were out of action. Electricity was cut off in many parts because the Resistance had destroyed the long-distance high-tension wires. Food was short, and the franc was inflated.

Pierre Mendès-France, de Gaulle's Minister for National Economy, urged on the General the need for drastic measures to restore France's economy. This Minister's idea was a new note issue under which the existing issue would be withdrawn, and eventually those handing in their notes would receive the new issue in exchange. The idea was that by depriving the black market and hoarders of their ready cash for a week or so the whole course of inflation would be halted.

De Gaulle was not ready to appreciate so technical a point as this. He had at the back of his mind the idea that such an arbitrary move might smack of dictatorship. He decided in the end to allow the question to be decided by his Minister for Finance, Pleven, and Mendès-France. It was to prove one of the few big and far-reaching mistakes he made between 1940 and the day of his retirement from public affairs in 1946. But his decision not to take personal action to curb France's economic trouble—in his defense it must be said that almost all political parties were opposed to the full adoption of the Mendès-France plan— meant that inflation continued unchecked. When, on November 4, 1944, a new loan brought in 164,400 million francs, two-thirds of which was completely new investment, it appeared that the Mendès-France plan was unnecessary. But de Gaulle did not realize the implications of the 40 per cent rise in wages given to the workers at the same time. In effect, it meant that the new loan had merely absorbed the extra purchasing power which the wage rise had provided.

There were also the loyalty trials to worry de Gaulle, with their exhibition of unbridled passion. There was the problem of the reform of the Constitution, and there was the question of French participation in the first meetings of the United Nations.

The municipal elections took place in the spring of 1945 —on April 29 and May 6. There was a strong swing to the Left compared with the prewar councils, and the Communists and Socialists won almost half of the 957 towns with populations over 4,000.

The end of the war in Europe on May 7 made it possible for de Gaulle to fix the general elections for October of that year. But before they took place the referendum that de Gaulle suggested was held on the question of whether the Third Republic should be brought to an end and the Assembly to be elected in October limited in its life and powers. It was a triumph for de Gaulle, for 95 per cent of the electors ignored the advice of the Center and Left-wing parties and voted for a Fourth Republic, and 66 per cent voted that the Assembly should be limited in its life.

On October 21 the Left-wing parties swept the country in the general elections. The Communists won 160 seats, the Socialists 142, and the M.R.P., the Left-wing party of Georges Bidault, captured 152 seats. The Right-wing parties won only 66 seats.

The Courts of Justice were sitting regularly and dealing with hundreds, even thousands, of cases—Pétain, who gave himself up on the Swiss border when Germany capitulated, being the first—but the Communists clamored for greater speed and heavier sentences. Yet from 1945 to the end of 1946, 125,000 cases were tried by the courts, and 40,000 people were sentenced.

Not the least of de Gaulle's worries was the professional quality of his administration. In the same way as he had had, in London, to build up a general staff of all components from the material which became available day by day, so at this time in France his civil service contained many leading officials whose only qualification was that they had been good Resistance fighters. It was not enough to cope with the problems of resettling 2,500,000 returned prisoners and deportees, building up the country's medical and health services, restoring the schools and restaffing them, rebuilding the armed services and implementing the decisions relative to nationalization. Yet, in addition to the steps taken in 1944, de Gaulle nationalized the vast Renault works, the Bank of France, and four credit banks, the gas and electricity undertakings, the largest insurance companies, and all types of mining and fuel before the end of 1945.

He had also to face continued trouble with his Allies. In the Middle East the end of the war in Europe was a sign for the Syrian nationalists to revolt, and de Gaulle sent in French troops to put down the trouble. Once more the British Government interfered at the wrong time. Churchill ordered de Gaulle to withdraw his troops, but the best that the General would agree to was to stop fighting and to order the French to remain in their positions. Again Churchill ordered the French troops out of the field and back to barracks, despite the existence of the agreement of 1941, which gave France the right to maintain order in Syria and the Lebanon. This interference in Syria was a damaging blow to France. It brought no good to Britain, who had to face the same situation in Palestine in 1948.

After the general election the National Assembly came together on November 7, but it was not until November 13 that de Gaulle was elected President of the Council. He had told the last meeting of the Provisional Assembly, "I have no ambition but to march at the head of France till she has taken back her destiny into her own hands. But I could not serve out my term if, in such a grave matter, I should see those who represent the comrades with whom I fought side by side separated from me"—this was in reference to the instability of French Governments and the suggestion of a single assembly with totalitarian powers, of which he disapproved. He had been greeted with jeers then by those who only a few months before had hailed him as their liberator.

The Communists had demanded the portfolios of War,

Home Affairs, and Foreign Affairs, but de Gaulle dismissed this without a second thought. The best he was prepared to do for the largest party in the Assembly was to offer Maurice Thorez the post of Vice-President of the Council without portfolio.

The Government was formed on November 22, 1945, de Gaulle's fifty-fifth birthday. He faced a stormy period of quarrels and intrigue between the various parties in the nation. And ahead of him, too, was the danger to French interests in Indo-China, where Communist Vietminh forces had Tonkin, Laos, and part of Annam under their control.

On January 7, 1946, de Gaulle left Paris with his wife for Antibes. It seemed that he was taking a few days' essential rest before tackling even more difficult and worrying problems. He returned from the south on January 15, and on the 20th called a special meeting of his Cabinet at the Ministry of War. "I have decided to resign my position as President of the Council," he told his colleagues simply. "My decision is final and irrevocable. I ask M. Vincent Auriol, as senior Minister of State, to supervise current business."

Then he rose from his chair and walked to the door without another word or backward glance. And as he went Maurice Thorez, the Communist, spoke up. "There is a departure which does not lack greatness," he said.

De Gaulle, in his few days of rest at Antibes, had thought over the whole question of the new Constitution. It had occurred to him that one thing stood in its way— his presence as President of the Council. He feared that the drafters of the new Constitution suspected that he had ambitions of dictatorship, and that therefore they would insert in the Constitution clauses which would make impossible a future strong President. He knew that the aim of his opponents was to ensure that the President of the Republic should always remain just a figurehead. In those days he often thought of a comment by Marshal Clauzel, famous French General of the Napoleonic War in Spain, "And now you are about to see the most difficult operation in the art of war—the retreat."

General Charles de Gaulle retired to the State-owned lodge at Marly-le-Roi. There, for days and weeks, he lived the life almost of a hermit within a house that was as closely guarded as any fortress in France. The most extraordinary precautions were taken, and the guards included detectives of the French Sûreté, members of the Garde Républicaine, the local police, and the armed services. A minute record was kept of the General's actions and visitors. His visitors included most often Gaston Palewski, his old-time assistant in London, for all the time he was working on his plan for a return to power if France should call for him.

Captain Claude Guy was the General's constant companion in those days. Together they took delight in outwitting the guards when they left the lodge. The policemen had been ordered to keep out of sight, but not to lose sight of the General. "Often he will double back on us and meet us face to face," one of the guards admitted. "Then he roars with laughter and walks back home. But at other times he will get well ahead of us, with his long legs, and turn off suddenly, so that we have no idea where he is."

The police kept a full log of the General's movements and those of his small staff. Thus: "Saturday, February 9, 1946. 1015: Cook shopping in village. 1500: General to Rambouillet [the neighboring town]. Sunday, February 10, 1050: General to Marly Church for Mass."

Throughout the spring de Gaulle continued to receive

French political leaders and public figures at Marly.
Palewski was a daily visitor. Juin, Chief of the Combined
General Staff, also came often to talk with de Gaulle. On
March 28 Vincent Auriol, the Socialist leader, who was
de Gaulle's successor, and Mme. Auriol went to Marly,
where the two men talked for hours, reviewing the whole
field of the political problems of France. De Gaulle urged
Auriol not to bargain away the French position on the
question of the separation of the Ruhr from Central Germany, it being widely believed at that time that Blum
intended to give way to the British and American pressure
to hand over the political control of the territory.

De Gaulle was in the best of spirits, and the glow of
health on his face showed that he was able to rest as he
had not rested for several years. As he always had done
whenever possible, he took long walks in the countryside
every day, and on these he thought out the problems of
the future months.

In the early summer he left Marly and went back to his
own home at Colombey-les-Deux-Eglises. There his life
followed the same pattern as it had at Marly.

Then, on June 16, 1946, he emerged from his home at
Colombey and travelled to Bayeux for the anniversary of
his visit there in 1944.

"The Constitution must give the Government the maxi-
mum of independence and cohesion, otherwise it will always be an organization without trust and divided against
itself," he told the assembled crowd. "France does not
need a dictator, for dictators lead to war, but she needs a
lower house elected by popular and free vote and a second
house to act as a check on it. Above both of these, elected
by the vote of the whole French Union, must be a President, removed from party loyalties, who would head the

executive, name the Premier and the Ministers, and, if there were a deadlock in the house, would have the power to dissolve Parliament and order new elections.

"Frenchmen, you must learn from history," he cried to the crowd, which had come from many parts of France to hear him. "Your entire history has always consisted of an alternative between the immense sufferings of a divided people and of great things achieved by a people united under a strong Government."

All this seemed like an admission that de Gaulle wanted to return to power by standing for Parliament. On September 18, when the leaders of three political parties—Socialists, Catholic M.R.P., and Radical—led by Vincent Auriol, President of the Constitutional Assembly, visited him at Colombey to beg him to clarify his own position in view of the dangerous situation that the rise of support for de Gaulle posed for France, de Gaulle denied any thought of returning to the political scene. "I disown the Gaullist Union," he declared. "I deny the story that I am preparing to back candidates at the coming elections, and I utterly dissociate myself from any policy of personal power."

After this there was a lull in the speculation as to whether de Gaulle intended to come back into the political arena. But on February 27, 1947, while on his way to the Canadian War Cemetery at Bruneval, de Gaulle paused at Criquetot, in Normandy, sufficiently long to announce that he was "coming out of retirement soon to help carry on work that remains to be done for France."

On April 3 Paul Ramadier paid a midnight visit to de Gaulle at Colombey, and the next day the Cabinet issued an official statement on the visit. "The General intends to make political speeches, and he has an absolute right to freedom of speech just as any other French citizen, and

perhaps more so," commented Ramadier. "Even if he criti-
cizes the Government it is our duty to protect his right
to do so."

De Gaulle had told Ramadier at their late-night meeting that he was determined to work until France had been
given a Constitution which would rid her once and for all
of the pernicious effects of party bickering and maneuvering.

Just four days later at Strasbourg de Gaulle announced
his program, which was based on the association of capital
and labor with a view to achieving increased production,
a stable currency, and the ending of the class struggle.
"The time has come to form a Rally of the French People,
to launch a great united effort to win our national salvation, to bring about reform of our Constitution, and to
triumph by constitutional means over our differences of
opinion," he said.

The Rassemblement du Peuple Français (R.P.F.) was
formed one week later in Paris, and Jacques Soustelle, the
former Minister of Information, became its organizing
head as Secretary-General. To assist him he had André
Malraux, René Pleven, André Le Troquer, André Diet-
helm, Paul Giacobbi, former Colonial Minister, who had
coined the description "French Union" in place of French
Empire, and Louis Jacquinot.

There was immediately an outcry from the Left that
de Gaulle was being financed by Fascists, who wished to
see a dictatorship installed in France.

On April 15 de Gaulle issued a statement to the press:

> Every Frenchman knows that in the present situation the fate
> of the country, and of every citizen, is at stake. Every Frenchman
> believes that if economic prosperity, social justice, imperial unity,
> and influence abroad are to be guaranteed—without which we

may lose the very liberty of each individual citizen and the independence of France—the whole country must unite in a pro-
longed and mighty effort of recovery. . . .

Every Frenchman feels that the present system must make way
for another, in which executive power proceeds from the country,
not from political parties, and irreconcilable conflicts are ap-
peased by the people itself.

The Rally of the French People is officially created to-day. I
assume its leadership. Its purpose is to promote the union of our
people and the reform of our State over and above national division.

Within a month the membership of the R.P.F. was more
than 750,000. Six months later it polled 2,000,000 votes in
the municipal elections for the urban seats alone.

But things went from bad to worse for France throughout the summer of 1947. By October, when de Gaulle's
Rally became the strongest single party in France—if the
municipal voting figures may be taken as a guide—there
was almost open talk of civil war in the country. At that
moment de Gaulle demanded an immediate dissolution of
Parliament, and on Vincennes racecourse addressed the
largest crowd ever to attend a political meeting in Paris,
when 500,000 people cheered him to the echo and
shouted, *"De Gaulle au pouvoir!"*

For a brief moment then it seemed that de Gaulle would
be sent for and asked to take control in an effort to keep
down the rocketing prices. Jules Moch, the Socialist who
had been made Minister of the Interior, asked Georges
Boris to stand by to carry a message to de Gaulle asking
him to take over the country. But Moch hesitated too long,
and, when immediate danger of a nationwide strike had
passed, he realized that the country would not accept an
arbitrary appointment of a man who was not even a Member of the Assembly.

There was crisis for the family at La Boisserie, Colombey-les-Deux-Eglises, as 1948 opened. Anne de Gaulle was sinking, and her parents realized that nothing could now prolong her life for more than a few weeks. Yet no one outside the immediate circle of the family was given any inkling of the trouble. Anne died on February 8, and so well had de Gaulle kept his sadness and worry from the outside world that his nonappearance in Paris for his weekly visit was put down to an admission of his political failure.

On March 7 de Gaulle made two speeches, one at Beauvais, the other at Compiègne, fifty miles northeast of Paris, where the armistice of the 1914-18 war had been signed, and where Hitler had insisted that the signing of the 1940 armistice with Pétain should take place. "As far as I am concerned, everything is ready to guide the country in the direction of salvation and greatness as soon as conditions allow," he declared.

But by June the call had not come. The London agreements on Germany, allowing the West Germans to establish a Constituent Assembly, gave him the chance of attacking the Government again. "The proposed [German] Constituent Assembly will become a Reich, and then nothing can stop the Russians setting up another Government at Leipzig," he said. "If the struggle that will then go on between these two groups in Germany and between the Powers, as a result of this rivalry, does not lead soon to war, one can at any rate guess which of these two Reichs will be sufficiently tough and rigid within itself and powerfully supported from abroad to win the day.

"Britain would traditionally welcome the renaissance of a Reich, so that in Western Europe, France and Germany would offset each other, with Britain as the umpire," was de Gaulle's opinion.

Still the political parties played their games against each other, and still France drifted. On August 29 *L'Aurore*, the Paris Right-wing Radical newspaper, urged France to

call for de Gaulle before the crash, or you will have to do it after it. De Gaulle is the only man capable of ending the political crisis [after the resignation of yet another Government—that of André Marie]. In the great hours of our history when everything seems lost France gathers herself together under the leadership of a chief. In 1917 the balance of the sword wavered; Clemenceau forged victory. In 1926, as to-day, the franc fluctuated; Poincaré restored confidence. . . . General de Gaulle has the same title as Clemenceau and Poincaré to be called the man who is able to rally the French.

Will the Deputies sacrifice their partisan prejudices to the high interest of the nation?

They would not. Although millions of Frenchmen were convinced that only de Gaulle could save the country, no call went out for him.

When November came and the country went to the polls in the elections for the Council of the Republic members of the R.P.F. and others pledged to support de Gaulle became the most powerful group in the Upper House. In March 1949 the party won a great success in the departmental elections. But the major political parties were by now so adept at maneuvering the coalitions of power that there was no possibility that de Gaulle would be called upon to return. And the General, immersed in writing and in his work for the new Anne de Gaulle Foundation for backward children which he and his wife had decided to found as a memorial to their daughter, made no apparent attempt to alter the situation.

Yet there was still the weekly visit to Paris to the Hôtel Lutétia, and to his office in the rue de Solférino, which was never closed. And, unknown to most Frenchmen, the leading figures of France still kept in the closest touch with the General, whose faith was still strong that one day the country would call for him.

Meanwhile he and his wife lived the country life and enjoyed it. De Gaulle was up every morning before eight, and his wife served him his coffee and fresh rolls in the dining-room. Then, rain or fine, they both set out on a walk through the gardens, before the General went up to his study in the tiny turret to sit at his desk, on which there was always a blotter engraved with the Cross of Lorraine.

There were only three servants at La Boisserie—Philomène, the cook, Louise, the maid, and René, the General's chauffeur, who drove his battered Citroën. A gardener, Jacques Roux, came in from the village to tend the garden and its huge flower Cross of Lorraine.

De Gaulle realized after some months that the R.P.F. had ceased to be an effective force in French political life. It had become just another political party needing to maneuver for position in order to keep itself alive. So, as the months and the years passed, the power of the R.P.F. steadily declined. In the 1951 elections only 118 of the Rally's candidates were elected to the Assembly, when a minimum of 180 were necessary to give it power. In the summer of 1952 a third of the R.P.F. Deputies seceded to form a new Parliamentary group. In January 1953, when his party voted René Mayer into power, de Gaulle told them that they might no longer use his name.

De Gaulle had declared that he supported the claim of Western Germany to the right to have a national army. He was pursuing his idea that the common Army for Europe was wrong, and that each country should maintain its own forces. "France will be sufficiently safeguarded if the political union of European States, including Germany, is formed and members are pledged to a common foreign policy," he maintained.

De Gaulle's plan was for a political confederation which would work according to three rules: no member would attempt to extend existing national territory by military force; no member nation would undertake any military action of any kind against any nation in Europe without prior agreement of all other members; Germany would agree that in peacetime she would have no more divisions than France, excluding those which France needed for her overseas territories.

De Gaulle visualized the Confederation as France, Germany, Italy, Holland, Belgium, and Luxembourg (the six nations which now form the Common Market group). France would enter this confederation as a single unit with the French Union in order to establish equilibrium with Germany and prevent German domination.

The General felt that every person with a vote in every member state should have the right to vote in a referendum on whether his own country should enter such a confederation. If the confederation were kept to the essentials of foreign, economic, and military policy the General felt it would lead to greater integration of the member states.

He was convinced that such a European political confederation was essential to remove the age-old Franco-German rivalry and to make possible genuine military collaboration.

The R.P.F. suffered a serious decline in the municipal elections of April 1953, and a few days later de Gaulle issued a statement that the R.P.F. would dissociate itself from political action and all its members in Parliament would, from that time, be free agents. But the R.P.F. would continue to exist, and the General made it clear that he was adopting new policies.

When the official ceremonies marking the tenth anniversary of the landings in Normandy were held in June 1954 de Gaulle refused the invitation to be present. Instead he went to the tomb of the Unknown Warrior under the Arc de Triomphe, and he and his followers stood in "absolute silence." It was made obvious that this was a gesture of protest against the European Army and French Government policy.

He had for long been of the opinion that international Communism could not succeed in the long run in dominating the world unless by force of arms or by an apparent overwhelming strength of arms. Therefore he had sought a *détente* with Russia, and he argued that the criterion of that *détente* should be the limitation of armaments and a controlled ban on atomic weapons.

Throughout the year 1954 he was outlining his ideas on the French Union. In April he drew attention to the fact that France had in Europe, in Africa, in the Indian Ocean and the Pacific, positions without which the fate of the West would be seriously compromised, and from which, if need be, the fate of the East could without doubt be sealed forever.

"We have handed over our bases in Africa and Europe and have granted all the commands to the Americans without obtaining from them decisions on atomic war. Such a war could be conducted mainly from our bases without our having anything to say," he said, and left no one in any doubt that if he had remained in power the familiar de Gaulle intransigence would have seen to it that France obtained better terms from the Americans.

In December 1954 de Gaulle said that for North Africa he envisaged a combination embracing Metropolitan France and French Africa in which the only authority is the French. "I envisage a combination in which defense and external affairs devolve upon France and consolidate with France the 100,000,000 inhabitants of the area, a combination whose positive actions are certainly in line with those of other Western systems, but for which its Ministers and generals are responsible before our country. That is what should be created," he argued.

From time to time the General emerged from his retirement to give widely publicized press conferences. On July 2, 1955, he declared that France should never have relinquished the guarantees she possessed in regard to German rearmament. "I believe, in particular, that, while accepting the principle of German rearmament, we should not have agreed to its implementation without a clear view of what Germany is going to do with it and without having pursued the Saar question to an end," he said. "A rearmed Germany will not cease to seek reunification, and this involves the risk that the West will be dragged along with it in order to seize this unity from the Soviets, or the risk that Germany will turn to the East in order to buy unity from them."

And so the months dragged by with the political situation in France gradually deteriorating. De Gaulle occasionally called for drastic changes in the French Constitution as a means by which some at least of the country's difficulties might be solved. And before the general elections in January 1956 he suspended the entire local organization of the R.P.F. throughout France, so that there could be no question of its being used politically.

It was not until 1957, when the troubles in North Africa took an even more serious course, that there was any real public call for the General's return. Then the Poujadist Party Congress at Strasbourg called on de Gaulle and Juin to give France a new lead. This was followed by a campaign by his own old supporters in Parliament for him to be brought back at the head of an "authoritative" Government to renovate France's political system.

De Gaulle made no move. He made no comment. He was waiting for the call that would be unmistakable. And that call did not come. The year ended, and 1958 was begun. And in the garden of La Boisserie at Colombey de Gaulle said to one of his closest friends, "I had hoped that I should be called last year. Now I begin to fear that it is too late."

19

Unity through Leadership

❧ The followers of de Gaulle had been given many lessons in the value of intransigence adopted at the right time. But the General soon showed that the methods he used to carry out his plans were not necessarily to be delegated to his supporters. This was particularly impressed on the colonists in Algeria. They were restive under restraint, and too many of them imagined that because they had carried the General to power on their own intransigence with authority they could continue to wield that power in the life of France.

On June 10, 1958, the Committee of Public Safety in Algiers passed a unanimous resolution, addressed to de Gaulle, who had come to power on June 1, in which they declared that they opposed the holding of municipal elections until a referendum had been held. They demanded the abrogation of the Algerian outline law (defining the relationship of Algeria with Metropolitan France), which had been passed by Gaillard's Government. The Committee further called for the complete integration of Algeria with France, and also for the abolition of all political parties.

De Gaulle was not greatly put out by this display of force. He had expected it, and he was equally prepared to reject the demands. He realized that there was nothing more vital for France than the solution of the Algerian problem. Therefore he replied to the Committee of Public Safety's demands with a brusque telegram to Salan in which he said that he took an entirely unfavorable view of them. He described them as "peremptory." "I remind you that your Committee has no right or role other than that of expressing under your supervision the opinion of its members. The official authorities, and in the first place you yourself, cannot have any part in what this Committee or any other political organization may voice or ask," he said.

Three days later de Gaulle broadcast to the people of France and asked them to have faith in their future, to cast aside "the spirit of Mephistopheles" and follow instead "the spirit which drives everything forward along the road which is a hard but a fine one."

Behind the scenes there were many difficult moments between de Gaulle and the Committee of Public Safety in Algeria, and almost as many with the militant section in France itself, who held the same views as the Committee. But de Gaulle, in the years which he had spent out of power, had learned a great deal about the diplomatic handling of men. Observers said that he had mellowed, but it would have been truer to say that he had profited from his reflections while out of office, and had realized that holding power in peace was a much more difficult job than retaining it in war. He was still authoritative—if that can be construed as being something less than dictatorial—in his dealings with his subordinates, but he was more prepared to be patient with those who were not able to appraise a problem with his own swift brilliance.

He had not changed in his conduct of administrative matters. He was still a bad "office man," still not prepared to take time over matters which he felt were of minor

importance, but he was more prepared now to listen to
the viewpoints of others on those problems which were
vital to France.

As soon as he took over the post of President of the
Council in 1958 he took control of foreign affairs, and he
busied himself with a full review of France's defenses. Yet
he managed to spend considerable time in furthering the
work of the Anne de Gaulle Foundation. The Foundation
maintains a home for backward children in a lovely house
in the valley of the Chevreuse, and the General and Mme.
de Gaulle provide all the funds out of their private income. The home itself is run by Mother Madeleine and the
Sisters of Calvary, but the General and his wife are fre-
quent visitors.

In his office at the Hôtel Matignon de Gaulle might still
have been preparing a military exercise. Everything he
did was run on the lines of a military campaign—every
next move thought out and every countermove of the
other side considered and placed in position in the over-all
plan.

Almost at once the General declared that France was to
be an atomic Power in full equality with the United States,
Russia, and Britain. He prepared the rough draft of a
defensive scheme for France in the future. Once again de
Gaulle realized that the wheel has turned, and that the
methods of the latter part of the last war are as outmoded
as were those of the 1914-18 War in 1939. To-day de Gaulle
thinks of defense in terms almost of fixed defenses of the
Maginot Line type, combined with mobile armies equipped
with the most modern weapons. France must possess
atomic weapons, but he does not believe that these alone
will prove decisive in any future war. He believes that
the man and individual weapons are still most important.

He does not visualize the use of the great and somewhat cumbersome armored divisions that he did so much to bring into being. His division will be light and fast-moving, capable of taking advantage of a tactical situation achieved by atomic weapons, and flexible enough to carry on static warfare in the periods of stalemate.

But de Gaulle's time was taken up more often with the pressing matters of France's economic troubles. Algeria was keeping almost half a million French soldiers under arms, and the cost was crippling. De Gaulle still believed that the solution of France's economic difficulties could be achieved swiftly if only the Government had the power to take the most drastic and unpopular measures.

His work was prodigious in amount. He was handling questions connected with almost every department of the Government. On July 29 he published the Draft Constitution while he was planning a great tour of French overseas territories and preparing for the elections of September. He left for Madagascar on August 20, and before he returned to France he had covered more than 13,000 miles.

On September 14 the Federal German Chancellor, Konrad Adenauer, travelled to Colombey at the invitation of de Gaulle, who was determined that France and Germany should find a common viewpoint on all major problems of Europe. He was still convinced that the peace of Europe was more a matter of good Franco-German relations than of those between Germany and Britain. He was anxious that France should take the lead in Europe, and he saw no reason why friendship and closer political and economic ties with Germany should not come as a result of French initiative.

France went to the polls on September 28 to vote on the matter of the new Constitution. All ninety Departments of

Metropolitan France voted "Yes," with 17,668,790 votes as against only 4,624,511 "Noes." Of the 84.8 per cent of the electors who voted, 79.15 per cent voted for the new Constitution. The following day the overseas territories voted almost as conclusively. Algerians went to the polls in greater strength than ever before: no less than 80 per cent of the electorate voted, and the percentage of "Ayes" was 96. Only French Guinea of all the overseas possessions voted for independence.

By October de Gaulle was beginning to show his restiveness over the North Atlantic Treaty Organization as it related to France. On October 25 he wrote personal letters to Eisenhower and Macmillan and an *aide-mémoire* to fourteen other NATO member countries suggesting three-power talks on NATO among France, Britain, and the United States. It was a sign that the path of the NATO planning would no longer be as smooth as it had been in the past, and that de Gaulle would soon be insisting on taking a much more prominent part in the Organization than anyone in France had taken since it was set up.

The elections of November 30 throughout Metropolitan France swept the U.N.R. (Union for the New Republic, the new Gaullist party) into power in the Assembly with 189 seats. This success led naturally to the acceptance by de Gaulle on December 13 of the invitation to stand for President. His opponents were Georges Marrane, a Communist, and Albert Châtelet, of the Union of Democratic Forces. The result in this indirect election was a foregone conclusion. De Gaulle received 62,394 votes, Marrane had 10,354 supporters, and Châtelet polled 6,722 votes.

It was January 8, 1959, when de Gaulle moved from the Hôtel Matignon, where he had lived as President of the Council, to the Elysée Palace, where he would rule as

President of France. There President Coty declared: "French people have recovered their unity through the General's leadership. For the first time in history a revolution has been carried out calmly and with full respect for the laws that it was the main purpose to change."

There could have been few more striking tributes to the leadership of de Gaulle. There were, even then, signs that a good proportion of the country did not support his policies, yet the majority of Frenchmen believed that only he could save the country from disaster, or at least that his leadership was the only choice open to them.

The new President's working day for the next few months was longer and more arduous than it had ever been in his life. Yet, at the same time, those who were most intimately connected with him realized that the General had indeed mellowed and was now less of a coldly reasoning machine. He would start the day with a reference to the weather, to the health of the person he was dealing with at that moment, even comment on some normally trivial happening that had made the newspaper columns that day.

On March 25 he revealed once more his determination to draw closer to West Germany. On that day, at his first press conference since taking over the Presidency, he opposed any policy of disengagement in Central Europe. "If the zone of disarmament or disengagement did not go as far towards the Urals as it went towards the Atlantic, France would not be covered," he said.

"Germany threatens us in no way. We even consider that with her capacities and resources she could produce an essential element of the life and progress of Europe and the whole world. France and Germany are determined to cooperate. On this point the policy of Chancellor Adenauer coincides with our policy and with that of Italy.

"We shall therefore support nothing which can push the German people to despair, compromise their peaceful future, or ruin the hopes which after so many shocks and fears have been raised on both sides of the Rhine."

Here was the fulfillment of the real theories of his early books, the results of his many painstaking surveys of Germany and the German character. Here were fruits perhaps of that almost forgotten book *La Discorde chez l'ennemi*, in which he had tried to analyze the faults of both Germans and French.

This was the first press conference ever held at the Elysée Palace. The President sat in the Banqueting Hall, and had with him every member of his Cabinet. For twenty minutes he spoke without notes and without hesitation to the five hundred journalists present.

"France will oppose any recognition of the East German Government," he said emphatically. "We are not disposed to recognize the Pankow System as a sovereign and independent State, because the system has been brought into existence and continues to exist only by virtue of the Soviet occupation and thanks to an implacable dictatorship.

"Reunification of the two parts of Germany is the normal destiny of the German people, provided the German people do not question their present frontiers with the West, the East, the North, and the South."

The President did not specifically mention the Oder-Neisse Line between Poland and East Germany, but it is his belief that an acceptance of that frontier by the Western Powers could form an important bargaining element in any negotiation with the Russians.

De Gaulle told his listeners that because France did not yet possess the atom bomb she could regard the international situation with a more detached view than could the other Great Powers who did have the bomb. "But

France would not try to stand aside in any conflict on this account," he said. "For France to attempt to keep outside a conflict or an eventual war would be tantamount to France losing her reason for living.

"It would mean annihilation of the Atlantic Alliance, which is inconceivable unless France is a part thereof. Without the Atlantic Alliance there would be nothing, barring an atomic war, to prevent Soviet domination extending itself over the whole of Europe and the whole of Africa until it covered the whole world," he said.

"France prefers to maintain the Atlantic Alliance until the day when the future of peace is really assured."

It was inevitable that the President would turn to Algeria. "Algeria's destiny will be decided by the way she votes, and I am sure, without wishing to prejudice the future, that the Algerians wish their fate to be linked with that of France, because this is in conformity with common sense and with prevailing sentiment," he said.

There were important pointers to the way the President was thinking and planning in this press conference. Behind the scenes de Gaulle was working out the first moves in his plan to bring a greater unity to Europe: he was convinced that this alone could bring safety from Russian expansionist programs. Algeria, he knew, was the key to the whole problem. If that problem could be solved, then France could indeed lead Europe politically and economically.

But there was little real sign that the rebels in Algeria, any more than the colonists, were ready to accept peace and equality. The sporadic raids continued, and there was still a need for the utmost vigilance on the part of the French Army.

At the end of April de Gaulle allowed it to be made

known, in a report of a conversation between himself and the editor of the *Echo d'Oran*, that he would not accept the word "integration" in Algeria, because that word had been consistently forced on him. Yet what else had he ever in fact carried out in the country besides integration, he asked. Since the end of the war he had striven to bring the Moslems and the colonists together. He had given the vote to the Moslem community of Algeria, and since his return to power had used all his efforts towards assuring respect for the legal equality of every one—the same voting rights and the same access to public office not only in Algeria, but also in France. "The Constantine Plan aimed at a vast depauperization of Algeria," declared the President. "Is not that real integration?"

There was considerable surprise in some quarters on May 18 when the Secretary-General of the Union for the New Republic—the party which numbers both Michel Debré, the French Premier, and Jacques Soustelle among its members—announced that de Gaulle was the "clandestine chief" of the party. "Things must be recognized as they are," Albin Chalandon revealed in a report. "General de Gaulle is our clandestine chief, and we are rather in the position of secret agents who owe total obedience to their military chief, who does not hesitate to disavow them when things go badly."

Debré at the same time issued a statement on Algeria which presumably was intended to carry the stamp of de Gaulle:

"As far as Algeria is concerned, we must act so that at the end of the year 1959 there will be no longer any chance for the rebellion to impose not only its military views, but equally its political views.

"The three main aims of our policy are (1) pacification

—that is to say, constant effort against everything that is the rebellion in Algeria and in Metropolitan France; (2) evolution—that is to say, economic transformations, Moslem social advancement, and the affirmation that those of the Europeans of Algeria who want, by some sort of incomprehensible nostalgia, to go back to the Algeria of the past twenty years, are in no way our supporters, any more than we are theirs; (3) the affirmation of French legitimacy—that is to say, the administrative, judicial, and economic presence of French administrators—by the effort that we are going to make in men and in credits, so that there can be no doubt that only France can achieve the transformation of Algeria."

De Gaulle, on his third visit to the French provinces since he returned to power, had said on May 7 at Bourges: "Without promising any date, without advancing any promise, I can say after due reflection that the day is in sight when Algeria will be pacified." De Gaulle drew attention to the fact that "French institutions have been changed for the better, and must now be made to work in practice. The signal for the change came from Algeria a year ago, but there would have been nothing but civil war and anarchy if the whole nation had not also pronounced in favor."

But all was not well in France. The opposition to the austerity programs of the new Government was growing, and de Gaulle had to promise to relax some of them—particularly income tax—in an effort to keep the workers in some measure of restraint. These cuts in tax, ranging from 12½ per cent for bachelors to 20 per cent for a married man with two children, began to operate in 1960.

His new-found friendship with West Germany, France's leadership in the Common Market of Europe, and the success of his visit to Italy, which showed that he had firmly brought the wartime Axis allies to the side of France, were all signs that politically and diplomatically he was having somewhat more success than he was economically. Yet the economy of France was improving, and there was increasing resilience in trade statistics.

That de Gaulle should find it possible to come out openly against the influence of the United States in NATO was a sign that he not only felt it was essential that he should make his stand against the atom-carrying bombers flying from French bases, but that he believed that France was fully strong enough to make herself heard and understood despite the opposition of America and Britain.

The wartime role of General de Gaulle, as far as America and Britain were concerned, seemed to be re-enacted. "Intransigence" was again a word used to describe the General's attitude, just as it had been during the war. But de Gaulle has always found great benefits in intransigence, and he has not changed either his beliefs or his policies since that time. It is still "De Gaulle for France."

In almost everything he did and said there was the idealism of the young de Gaulle. It was probably no coincidence that his first social act as President was to attend the Annual Ball at Saint Cyr Military Academy on January 31, 1959. "I rediscovered my youth," was his only comment at the end of the evening. And when a fortnight later he went to Toulouse, the scene of some of the fiercest opposition to his ministry and presidency, he was greeted by large and enthusiastic crowds. His word for them was, "I will make a promise to you and to the rest of France. This year will be difficult for each of us and for all of us together. But after that the gates of progress will open wide."

Undoubtedly he had in mind the great French gas and oil fields and the developing might of the Sahara. He visited the Sahara in December 1958, and at Touggourt declared, "The Sahara will become the great link between the Mediterranean world and Black Africa, and between the world of the Atlantic and that of the Nile and the Red Sea.

"France has a direct interest in this immense task. She accepts this work, and wishes to bring it to a successful conclusion. She needs for this the support of all, and notably that of the peoples of the Sahara."

It was because he was not afraid to make forthright pronouncements on matters most vital to France that his prestige in France, despite occasional rumblings of opposition, was in fact enhanced as the days went by. Thus a strongly worded resolution criticizing de Gaulle which was proposed at the annual conference of the French Socialist Party at Issy les Moulineaux, a Paris suburb, on July 12 was overwhelmingly defeated.

He went to Algeria again in August, and on August 29 at Tebewsa, Eastern Algeria, promised a "new era" to the country, once pacification was achieved. Tebewsa is close to the Tunisian border and it has seen a great deal of the activity of the Algerian rebels. De Gaulle told his listeners that the first thing that must be won in Algeria was peace.

"Afterwards a new era will begin," he said. "It has already begun for France. It will open for Algeria. The Algerians will decide their destiny for themselves. That is a necessity. Difficulties and delays certainly remain to be overcome. What counts in the end is the goodwill of men."

On October 15, 1959, the French Assembly, voting on the President's plan for Algeria, gave de Gaulle what amounted to a free hand to proceed. The voting was 441 in favor, as against 23 opposed, with 28 abstentions and 57 absentees.

Still, his first thought is the greatness of France—not in terms of military grandeur or economic splendor, but in terms of acts and policies. To de Gaulle the glory of France in the past was its humanizing ability; the greatness of the Empire was measured in terms of the development of the underdeveloped people. To him the pacification of Algeria is not a desire for military triumph, but a demonstration that a Moslem people can freely choose French institutions because they are the best. To him the development of the wealth of the Sahara is worthwhile only if it raises the living standards of both French and Moslem to equal levels.

De Gaulle dreams of a France which will be looked up to by the world as a worthy and natural leader.

Index